Case Histories of Tentmakers

Edited by

James L. Lowery, Jr.

Morehouse-Barlow Co., Inc.
Wilton, Connecticut

©1976 Morehouse-Barlow Co., Inc.
78 Danbury Road (Rte. 7)
Wilton, Connecticut 06897
ISBN-0-8192-1216-4

Printed in the United States of America

PREFACE

A. Donald Davies

Devout church people have always prayed for the increase of the ministry. But we do not know what to do with God's answer to our prayers. An abundance of persons have responded to the Lord's call, and the church now has a surplus of clergy, in many areas. For the first time in history, the American Episcopal Church has more clergy than there are cures and vacancies.

For many the response to this surplus is simple: Cease accepting candidates. This response, however, raises serious theological questions. The real problem is not how to stave off the increase in numbers, nor how to reduce the surplus. The problem is how can the church utilize those called by God to the ministry. Perhaps the surplus concept says a great deal about our dim vision of the mission Christ has entrusted to us. It also speaks of the church's limited understanding of the opportunities to exercise a variety of ministries in our day.

It is providential that as the surplus was growing, a significant direction for new ministry also emerged. The ancient tentmaker priest has stepped forward with twentieth century apron and tools. What a few timid clergy had tried quietly (often secretly) began to take on new dimensions and authority. Thus our Lord has launched again in our time a most exciting and renewing venture for ministry. It is to be seen in the freedom discovered by clergy who are developing creative lifestyles and ministries as they labor in a secular vocation.

Not long ago, church people suspected any clergyman not laboring in a parish church on a full-time basis. There was a shadow of doubt about his character, ability, and commitment. After all, he had given up the ministry! Thus it went. But our Lord has led us to recognize the place and function of the tent-maker priest, or worker priest, or non-stipendiary priest. Rather than being suspect, such an exercise of ministry is now growing both in numbers and respectability throughout the country.

The exercise of this "new" form of ministerial relationship is different from the more familiar and conventional form in several ways. First, to dedicate one's major time and concern in the workaday world through a secular job requires special skills, competency, and talent in addition to theological training. Not all of us can qualify. Second, the competitive world is the arena in which the tentmaker's stewardship and servanthood are tested, evaluated, and rewarded. Third, dependence upon church finances is no longer necessary. But in many ways through this new lifestyle the worker priest brings fresh insights and gifts to the local worshiping congregation he serves. Indeed, his basic role and function as a priest takes on new and creative dimensions. Such dual-vocational people find both personal fulfillment and new opportunities for ministry and witness to the Gospel.

One last word. Will the church accept the new directions? As a bishop, I recognize my worker priests as being as much an extension of my ministry as any priest who serves in a parish, a chaplaincy, a teaching post, or in a counselling ministry. It is a fully recognized, approved, and supported ministry equal with any others. The church must be made aware of the need to accept and include these adventurers in her comprehensive mission and ministry to the world. Therefore it is a privilege to be part of this venture, and to herald those who through this volume witness to Almighty God leading and prospering ministry to his glory and praise.

> Bishop's Office
> Episcopal Diocese of Dallas
> October 1975

FOREWORD
HOW THIS BOOK CAME TO BE

James L. Lowery, Jr.

This book is the corporate work of a network of self-supporting ministers and their friends across the ecumenical spectrum. While most are Episcopalians, the case histories are by no means limited to that denomination. The mushrooming of tentmaking ministries is evidenced by the fact that self-supporting clergymen now constitute twenty-two percent of the ordained personnel of the mainline Christian churches.[1] This style of ordained ministry, filling a church position on top of a secular financial base, is no longer just the property of sectarian Protestant and Pentecostal bodies. It is a historic form of ministry and was the norm in the first three or four centuries of church history.

There is at one and the same time, on the part of judicatories and churches, an acknowledgement of the "bi-vocational ministry" and an interest in it, but also an ignorance of its variety and breadth and a paucity of intelligent attempts at its deployment. This is due partly to fear of a diminished control over this "new type" personnel, most of whom have had to be nothing less than entrepreneurs and "hustlers" in order to put together the fascinating and creative combinations they describe in this book. Partly it seems due to ignorance of the varieties and different dynamics associated with different types of tentmakers.

This volume can be a help in dealing with such fear and ignorance, and is offered for use in seminaries, judicatories, congregational study groups, and perusal by groups of clergy. If there is sufficient desire, the editor is willing to produce, on relatively short notice, a study guide for use with the book. But at this point it is felt the volume itself will provide wide stimulus without additional "discussion questions."

The basic idea of this study came out of the life of the National

Association for the Self-Supporting Active Ministry at one of its annual conferences at Roanridge Institute outside Kansas City, after a series of presentations by Dean Holmes, author of the Introduction. Some of the writers of case histories which follow were also present. We accepted the task of collecting and editing the material which could be found. The Episcopal Diocese of Dallas graciously made a subvention towards publication, and Morehouse-Barlow consented to be the publisher.

The mailing list of NASSAM was solicited for case histories in 1974-75. The respondents, and suggested friends, produced rough draft case histories. Effort was made to include men and women; an ecumenical sampling; rural, suburban, and urban situations; large and small congregations; and special settings. We also looked for a geographical balance among the various sections of the country, as well as abroad. Fervent thanks go to the several dozen persons who worked hard on case histories, and a special word to those who furnished studies which could not be published due to duplication of subject or lack of space.

The case histories are intended to answer the following questions:

1. What do you do, and how did you get into this arrangement?
2. How does your ordained state affect you in doing your secular job?
3. What have you learned from the secular setting of your job that affects ministry?
4. How does your secular job itself affect your church ministry?
5. How does being a tentmaker affect the parish church setting you are in?
6. What other conclusions would you draw about ministry from your experience?

The case histories were divided into fifteen full-sized studies, and nine mini-histories. The first draft edition of these was circulated throughout the same tentmaker-support mailing list for suggestions, changes, and feedback. After the case histories had been read, Dean Holmes produced the Theological Introduction, Bishop Davies the Preface, and we did the Foreword and Epilogue. With all the joint effort involved, it is now offered as a practical aid to church ministry in the last quarter of the twentieth century.

The editor is acutely aware of the help rendered by many people without which this work could not have appeared. In addition to the case history authors and Dean Holmes of Sewanee, as well as Bishop Davies of Dallas, we owe special thanks to Mr. Ronald Barlow and Miss Margaret Sheriff of Morehouse-Barlow, Inc., the Rev. David Works of the North Conway Institute, and the swift competence at the typewriter of Mrs. Helen Corrigan. Anita and Monique Lowery have put up with much time stolen from them to write and edit. The Christian fellowship is truly a supportive one.

Cambridge, Massachusetts
October 1975

INTRODUCTION

Urban T. Holmes

The customary understanding of the non-stipendiary ordained ministry is to think of it as a compacted version of the stipendiary or full-time parish pastorate. The kind of questions we ask reveal our own prejudice. How can the priest who works forty hours a week or more in a "secular" job find time to make calls, to counsel, to meet with parish committees, to represent the church in civic affairs, to produce the weekly bulletin, to visit in the hospitals, etc.? The assumption is that to be a priest or a deacon is *by the nature of ordination* to do all these things. What we have done is confuse the functions of ordination which are *central* to the office with those which are *occasional*.

In the research done from 1974-1975 by the Study Committee on the Preparation for the Ministry throughout the dioceses of the Episcopal Church, it was evident that this confusion exists generally. Whereas many dioceses have programs for the training of non-stipendiary clergy, bishops and others are quite ambivalent about the proliferation of the phenomenon. There is an uncertainty as to the quality of such persons, the fear that we are creating a "lower caste" in the clergy, a sense that they cannot do the job necessary, and a belief that the system is not geared for this type of ministry. Yet more than a third of the persons in training for ordination in the denomination now are being prepared outside of the accredited seminaries (400 out of 1100), and the majority of these (approximately 300) are looking forward to a non-stipendiary ministry!

Of course, the issue of non-stipendiary clergy is not unlike that of the ordination of women to the priesthood and what it means, not only in terms of its symbolic function, but also in terms of the more mundane job description. The former relates more clearly to the matter of women in the priesthood; the latter is raised by the presence of non-stipendiary priests.

I sense in the essays in this volume a struggle between what are the central functions in the job description of a priest or deacon and those which I would describe as occasional. Some priests, for example, speak of their need to find time to attend committee meetings or to call on newcomers, although there is less of this than I would have expected. On the whole, there is an effort, once the occasional duties of the ordained minister are sloughed off, to identify what in fact the priesthood or the diaconate is in essence, so that it is clearly understood what the non-stipendiary is as distinct from the non-ordained layman with whom he works. Here the struggle appears most acute, because we have confused the occasional with the central functions.

A clue to the possible resolution to this question lies in the frequent repetition, in a series of variations in a number of articles, of the one theme that the ecclesial vocation must not be lived in separation from the secular job. It is particularly true of the priest that he first *is*. He is the sacramental person, who by his life and stewardship of the church's liturgy, unveils for all the extraordinary presence of God *within* the ordinary. Some find this to be the real payoff of the non-stipendiary ministry; others are concerned about how they might realize their vocation to witness outside of the church walls and the predictable life of the parish to the presence of God within the common life of their associates. Whether or not the desired end has been realized, the sensitivity to the central function of the priest is on target.

The priest ideally is one who lives in the world, sees God's presence in all of life, and enables others to see. He does not call people to leave the world, but to live their daily lives in terms of a vision that gives hope to the routine business of survival. The priest holds before us the truth that all of life is *sub species aeternitatis* ("under the vision of eternity"). The Christian life is not esoteric in the sense that it is world-denying, even in the more subtle sense of that word. That is to say, there is no virtue in church sponsorship or the "baptism" of the ordinary life of man, in order "to make it holy."

This is a key point for our understanding of the non-stipendiary clergy. An illustration is in order. For over six years I was the semi-stipendiary priest of a small but very alive mission in the

Diocese of Milwaukee. I gave about eight hours a week to the ministry of that congregation. A few members complained, because they felt that if they had a full-time priest the church would then "be more active in the community." Perhaps there were good reasons for their complaints about my very part-time presence, but this was not a valid one. For either their complaint meant that by the priest "being active in the community" the *church* was active in the community, which is sheer nonsense, or they meant that a full-time priest would enable the members to be involved in the community "in the name of the church." Just how a full-time priest would do this I am uncertain. The fact of the matter was that (as a result of a survey of the congregation) it was evident that the forty or so adults in this mission were among the leaders in the community. In what way their Christian witness could be improved by labeling their participation with the name of the congregation escapes me.

The truth would seem to be that in our doctrine of ministry we have begun by accepting the departmentalization of the church, religion, and God which has evolved over the last two hundred years. The Christian faith is understood not so much as a perception of life which pervades our work, our family life, and our play, but it is an activity among other activities. The priest becomes somebody whose business is that isolated activity, and it is very difficult to see how he has any function outside of his "field." If something is to be considered Christian, it has to fall within the departmentalized activity, and it is the business of the professional leader of that department to supervise it.

When I was a university chaplain, I was not infrequently asked what I was doing teaching (particularly in clericals) in the foreign language department, why I was to be found on the side of the campus opposite the Episcopal center rather than in my designated pigeonhole, and for what cause I kept interfering in the "non-religious" affairs of the university. I say "asked." This inquiry was occasionally direct and confronting, but—more diabolical—it was often implicit and oblique. My reply was and still is that my most effective ministry to people was outside the confines of the center. It was during those ten years that I came to the firm conclusion that the priestly ministry within a university can most effectively be done by one who is identified with the staff or faculty of the institution itself as well as with the church.

What is in fact wrong with our doctrine of ministry and the source of some of our confusion between the central and occasional functions of the priesthood, in particular, is that we do not understand the Incarnation. The Word did not become a temple functionary, he became man! Jesus did not live out his life as a rabbi (although he was apparently called that from time to time) but as a Galilean peasant. It is all too easy to fall into the cult of the "common man" and give a romantic aura to the so-called "simple life"; but certainly the Incarnation was the in-flesh-ment of God within the ordinary life, at whichever socio-economic level we are considering.

There is a very natural tendency in western culture, particularly the modern northern European type, to fall into a kind of dualism. We separate the sacred and the profane, the natural and the supernatural, time and eternity, and we isolate God from his creation. On the contrary, Christian theology is clear that the profane always lies *within* the sacred, the natural *within* the supernatural, and time *within* eternity. All of creation is *within* God, even though God is infinitely more than creation. There is nothing that lies outside the presence of God, and in humanity's one and only way of knowing, God can be perceived in any part of his world.

If the non-stipendiary ministry is to be taken seriously, it confronts us with this truth. In fact, it calls us back to a time before the disenchantment of our world—say two hundred or so years ago—before there were full-time priests in our sense of the word (persons being paid a middle class salary for what they do, which is intended to support them—albeit at a marginal level—as professionals within a technological society), and when the hand of God was seen in every facet of life. In the essays in this book there is this implication, which is very exciting. Certainly the reality of a dissolution of the departmentalization of Christian faith is more potential than actual within these pages, but it is there. Take, for example, Bill Pollard's testimony on how he was forced to think through the relation of science and religion, or Harry Woggon's efforts to make his way among the emotionally disturbed without the southern Appalachian stereotype of "preacher."

This effort to focus the central functions of the priesthood and diaconate in the making visible of the extraordinary presence of God within the ordinary life is an immensely difficult task in a secular society. It is far more arduous than making parish calls, attending committee meetings, and even pastoral counseling. What this means is that the non-stipendiary priest, who would embrace such a vocation, needs to be *better trained*, not less educated, than the average full-time priest! This is, I think, contrary to our usual assumption. A second or third class education does not serve the positive contribution that the so-called worker-priest can make to the affirmation of the Incarnation.

It would be wrong to stand in judgment of given institutions or situations that cater to the education of the non-stipendiary clergy. But it is interesting that the best performance in the General Ordination Examinations (GOE) in 1975 was a person trained outside of the ten accredited seminaries of the Episcopal Church. It is hard to escape the impression, however, that we seem ready to settle for a less than rigorous training for a person if he or she professes the intention of exercising a non-stipendiary ministry. This needs to be overcome. Furthermore, it is essential that we find ways, such as theological education by extension, to tie in the professional direction of theological education (i.e., what goes on in the accredited seminaries) with diocesan programs to prepare persons for ordination. This needs to include the use of the GOE across the board, if for no other reason than that the exemption of candidates for a non-stipendiary ministry implies that they cannot be expected to measure up to the standards set for stipendiary clergy.

Of course, many non-stipendiary clergy come out of the accredited seminaries. Some of them will say, quite rightly, that they were not prepared adequately to make the necessary distinction between the central and the occasional functions of the ordained clergy and to ground the priesthood in a theological understanding of ministry. This presents a challenge to what we are doing in theological education per se. It is often true that we have allowed ourselves to be deflected from the theological basis of the ministerial priesthood and the functions of the priest as the enabler of the revelatory experience. We have failed to produce in our students the essential skills to reflect theologically on all of life. The occasional functions of administrator, therapist, consultant, community staffer, etc., sometimes appear to be the tail that wags the dog.

If the need to develop a model of ordained ministry which is less than the compacted version of the full-time parish pastorate is taken seriously, then it is also true that the heart of the training task is to assist the non-stipendiary priest or deacon to develop a spirituality that not only enables him to survive outside the support system of the parish, but also enables him to work effectively. This is one way of overcoming the simplistic notion that a pastoral ministry is a profession. What do I mean? Just after World War II the worker priest movement in France was offered as a possible model of effective evangelism among the working classes of that country. Widely heralded, it became a failure in the minds of some, including the papal curia. The priests were seduced, we were told, by the secularism of the age rather than converting the world to Christ. The insistence was that for a priest to survive he had to have the support and discipline of the ecclesiastical structures and must remain in a community where we knew what to expect of him as a professional.

Without debating that very brief analysis of the demise of the French worker priest movement, I do think it is especially true that the non-stipendiary clergyman has to be a person whose spiritual pilgrimage does *not* depend upon such constant institutional reenforcement. His symbols must be integral and integrated! External constraints are not going to work. I have no objection, for example, to the recitation of the daily offices, nor to daily or frequent presence at the Eucharist, although I have strenuous objections to those who suggest that this particular pattern is not only normative for all priests, but necessary for a deep spiritual life. It is a structure which has served well, but is not a possibility for every person who puts in forty hours a week at a job and then ten to twenty more in ministry to a congregation. There need to be some other options than saying your office to yourself, as a non-stipendiary priest would probably find necessary, or making the Eucharist at 6:30 A.M. or on the way home from work.

I am struck by the fact that there is very little mention in these essays of the problem of the spiritual life. I suspect that most of the authors share what I find in many full-time parish priests: an endemic guilt over the fact that their disciplined life of prayer and meditation has collapsed. I hope I am wrong. Whether or not I am, what needs to happen is for us to take another look at man as spiritual being, and maybe the source of the guilt will be lifted.

It is impossible to digest here what I have said elsewhere, particularly in a forthcoming book, *Ministry and Imagination* (Seabury, 1976), concerning the nature of a possible new understanding of spirituality. I can summarize the thesis of that study by saying that spirituality begins with a person's *intentionality*. If we are to see God we must wait upon God within the ordinary flow of life, consciously, expectantly, and without imposing categories. We need to recover the imagination that God gave us, to learn to die to our personal need to control our world, and to identify moments of transcendent experience natural to us all. We must become people of the story, living by the symbols of our Christian faith as they emerge from the events of everyday life. We need to discover our own "creative weirdness" and live into it.

Unfortunately, there is little of that theme in the articles within this volume. Working in our society does not promote anything but the opposite of such a life style. Yet there is something *asymmetrical* or *marginal* in the very fact that a priest punches a time clock, does quality engineering, works in a biology lab, or practices medicine. I sense this is something of what Carl Praktish is getting at in his eloquent statement. That marginality needs to be raised up and affirmed, in order that it might become the imaginative shock to open both the non-stipendiary clergy themselves and those with whom they live to the possibilities inherent within the routine of their daily existence. In other words, if a priest is a catalyst to a new consciousness, which is called "conversion," then he must not fit into the univocal old consciousness. He has to be a trigger to the ecstatic experience or, if you prefer, the vision of God's immanence in the ordinary. Therefore, the weirdness of the non-stipendiary, who does not fit our categories of either priest or layperson, ought to be celebrated.

What follows from this is that the non-stipendiary ordained ministry is not for the well intended, semi-trained, Christian enthusiast. It is not a substitute for a preferable form of pastor, the full-time, seminary educated person. It does embody the possible discovery for our time of a worldly spirituality, a sense of God's presence in the midst of the factory, office, and classroom, which is often lacking in the conventional and comfortable forms of parish ministry: It is a living witness to what is traditionally known as the "sacrament of the present moment." Because such a ministry is novel and pioneering, it demands the very best quality of persons with the most efficient training, who have searched their inner selves and found the God who supports their being and the being of others in every state of life.

This is not what we customarily think of when we conceive of the non-stipendiary ministry, nor is it what we are doing in promoting it. Many of us equate this movement with lifting up the indigenous leader, after the manner of Roland Allen,[2] or ordaining the "sacramentalist." I am not necessarily in opposition to that, but the notion that commitment is all it takes to be an effective priest outside the parish structures is grossly in error. Wherever the source of non-stipendiary priests and deacons, the screening and the education must be responsive to the incredible task that lies before them. I believe in attempting this task as something which needs to be done. This book testifies that it is being done and consequently it offers hope for the liberation of the church in America from the ghetto of departmentalized Christianity and docetic parish life.

It is, therefore, a misconception to think of the non-stipendiary ordained ministry, as some do, as an expedient in the face of a growing fiscal crisis pertaining both to marginal congregations and the rising costs of theological education. It is particularly erroneous to pursue the non-stipendiary ministry as a stop-gap and to continue to think of "real parish ministry" as before. The non-stipendiary pastorate is, if anything, a basic challenge to our easy conceptions of the theology of priesthood and diaconate, with the definition of central and occasional functions that emerge from that theology. It confronts as well the hidden issue of the spirituality of the clergy and the glib prescriptions of the traditionalists. It demands, as does the ordination of women, a whole new look at the inherited assumptions and structures.

If the non-stipendiary ministry is to succeed as a potent force within the life of the church, therefore, it has to be considered more than an expedient. As an expedient only, it will die. If it succeeds in calling the present ecclesiastical system—now only about seventy-five to a hundred years old—into question and in creating some changes, it will have salutory effect upon the church for generations to come that will far exceed any possible money saved.

St. Luke's School of Theology
University of the South
Sewanee, Tennessee

CONTENTS

1.
ECOLOGY AND PRIESTHOOD

Brendan J. Whittaker

*Episcopalian Brendan Whittaker is chief of
information and education for the Vermont Agency of
Environmental Conservation, Montpelier, and priest in
charge of Christ Church, Island Pond, Vermont. He is
past president of Vermont TAP Water Corporation
(a non-profit group which aids low income Vermonters
who lack running water) and a member of the Society of
American Foresters.*

For five days every week I work at a full-time job as chief of environmental information and education for the Vermont Agency of Environmental Conservation. On Sundays and in-between times, I am priest-in-charge of a small parish in the heart of Vermont's most remote rural area, the so-called "Northeast Kingdom." Finally, as time permits (never enough!) with the aid of a willing family (my wife, the mother of three children, is also a full-time teacher) we live on the land in a small farm in Vermont's north country producing much of our own food, lumber, maple syrup, and fuel (firewood). It is a busy life, one that is intensely satisfying to us and, we hope, is holy.

The route that took us here is a fairly typical one for a person who comes from another profession. I was born and raised in a rapidly urbanizing section of eastern Massachusetts and got an early appreciation of what bits of open and wild land were left behind by the developers. Having had college training as a professional forester, and after an Army enlistment, I went to work as a forester for the state of Vermont, a place that had always drawn me.

1

A deepening layman's conviction about faith and religion led to my going to the Episcopal Theological School at Cambridge, Massachusetts, where I wrote my master's thesis on the relationship of the church to conservation. After graduation and ordination, I subsequently spent seven years in the full-time parish ministry back in Vermont, in the Rutland area.

A growing conviction came, however, that I was now being called to other work: to be in the environmental movement on a more permanent basis. An opportunity, which I had previously turned down because I had felt that my parish work was not yet finished, presented itself again. I returned to state government work in July of 1973.

In that job, I am in the state agency which manages and protects Vermont's magnificent forests and waters, air and soil. My own work consists of coordinating the information and education efforts of the different professional natural resource fields in the agency. I work with people who are in natural resources work because they love it and have great dedication, and with the Vermont public which, by and large, has staunchly backed this small, relatively non-affluent, state's decisions to become a quiet yet determined leader in sane and careful use of its resources. It is a state where thought is given to those who will come here after us. It is good to be with people like this in such beautiful surroundings. But, while it may be good, is it the place for a priest to be?

To explain this in depth necessitates some understanding of the environmental movement itself and why I as a priest feel called to be part of it. The ecology movement, as it is called, at its base is concerned with how life will continue to be lived on an earth increasingly short of the most basic commodities: food, energy, and their supporting natural resources of soil, minerals, clean water and air, with more and more people competing for these all the time.

The largest task within the environmental challenge, however, is not the mass of technological changes brought on by the energy shortage, but rather is similar to a type of religious preaching, that is, the convincing of people who have been used to living one way that basic changes in their lifestyles are necessary. The

Christian Church needs to be part of this "quiet revolution."

Because I am also a priest, with theological grounding, as I work with the environment and the people it supports, I see the need to gently chide fellow Christians for the stubborn persistence among us of that most ancient heresy, the denial of the goodness of the material. Environmental educators are just now perceiving the depths of the separation which humanity has effected between itself and nature.

In another context, I now realize how deep a recovery Christians must make of their own "nature-roots," which centers around finding again the true meaning of the church's central doctrine, the Incarnation, the Word made flesh, and what this implies as to our perception of the total created world. How much we Christians have lost! "The religion of the Incarnate Word was (in the earliest days of Christianity) all too quickly attacked by an ascetic virus which undermined its natural elements in favor of the supernatural."[3] Thus one contemporary theologian describes the tragic situation of modern western man, who not only has largely abandoned the church but comes close to poisoning the earth as well. The major task of the environmentalist is to bring awareness, respect, and love for the earth. The American Indian had these things; we all must find them once again if we are to survive. A major task for the Christian environmentalist is to see that the church plays a role in that recovery.

My own present role in the priesthood has evolved to this: Because of my independent salary, I am able to minister to a small rural congregation which could not afford a full-time pastor. At the same time, I am able to be a professional environmentalist at the center of state government where natural resource decisions are made. Though my salary may be secular, it is membership in the church which enables me to bring the presence of a priest to that center. Clergy have long been present in such fields as education, law, medicine, agriculture (the monastics), and science. In a humble sense, I feel that I must not only bring the concerns of environmentalists to the church, but also that I have a part in bringing the Christian vision, including the life of prayer, to the environmental movement.

The nature of my present "call," then, is that of one who works full-time in a secular profession because of conviction that the church ought to be there. Conversely, each week at the altar I am privileged to be able to bring into a more direct focus the concerns of the past week: perhaps a hostile legislative committee, a troubled fellow-employee, an appointed official struggling with a difficult management decision. Beyond this, I have been bringing in prayer the earth itself: a threatened tract of land, a river marred by pollution, and, on the joyful side, praise for a winter sunrise, thanks for an October afternoon among sugar maples, rain, or a good snowstorm. I am reminded of Teilhard de Chardin and his priestly offering of the whole earth-planet as Eucharist, raised up in his vision as the Sacred Host, offered back to the Father.

A truism among Vermont farmers, woodsmen, and other people of the land is that one of the best things a person can do in a lifetime is to be a steward of his tiny corner of the earth, so that when it is time to turn it over to someone else, the land is in better condition than when he received it. Isn't this really the Christian vision, when you expand it a little? Life comes as a gift (grace), and during its course it is sustained by our own efforts, to be sure, but far more by the natural gifts of soil, water, air, and sun. Then, at life's end, we look back individually (and some day, when it is time for all human life to leave earth, the race will do this collectively) and reflect on just how carefully and well we have used the gifts we have been given. We can then, with Teilhard, symbolically hold up the earth which has been our home, and say with great joy and conviction, as our last earthly Offertory, "All things come of thee, O Lord, and of thine own have we given thee."

2.
SUPPORT IN TENTMAKING

William H. Dodge

Bill Dodge is presently Senior Systems Programmer for the Office of Computer Services at Rensselaer Polytechnic Institute and Assistant Pastor at State Street Presbyterian Church, Schenectady, New York. Parts of this history originally appeared in Monday Morning, *a weekly for pastors of the United Presbyterian Church.*

"After this he left Athens and went to Corinth. There he fell in with a Jew named Aquilla, a native of Pontus, and his wife Priscilla; he had recently arrived from Italy because Claudius had issued an edict that all Jews should leave Rome. Paul approached them, and because he was of the same trade, he made his home with them and they carried on their business together; they were tentmakers" (Acts 18:1-4).

The presence of self-supporting clergy within the Christian Church is hardly a new idea or experience. From the time of the New Testament there have been such persons serving in their own special ways. However, the tradition of self-support is clearly not the one the Constitution of the United Presbyterian Church in the U.S.A. speaks of directly or indirectly. All the portions of the Book of Order and the Book of Discipline which refer to clergy very obviously have in mind those fully supported by the local congregation or by the denomination. Our practice, also, as evidenced by articles in *Monday Morning* and other places, looks upon those who may be self-supporting as other than normal.

I say all this because for the past nine years, I have found myself in the position of being a self-supporting clergyman. All this started when I was faced with the necessity of leaving a situation in a local church which I did not fit into. As many know, it is almost impossible, in our Presbyterian system, to move quickly when you really want to. The best solution for me at the time seemed to be to find any job I could for the moment, rather than prolong the agony for either myself or the congregation. At first, I had no real notion of what this might lead to. Should I leave the church behind me, as so many seemed to be doing at that time? Or should I look for some specialized place within the establishment, a course followed by some others?

After two years of secular employment, spending much time trying to find a direction for my ministry, and having maintained my activity within the Albany, New York, Presbytery and its committees, I decided to see if there was some way I could continue to serve the local church. I approached the pastor of one of the churches in the presbytery and asked if there was some way I could work with him, on a part-time, voluntary basis, to add my particular talents to the work of the church. Thus began on a tentative basis what has become a very rewarding ministry. I spent five years with that particular congregation, serving as stated supply and then assistant pastor. While I was there I had the opportunity to work with three different pastors of the church and several other pastors in neighboring congregations on cooperative efforts. After that period, I left that church for another in the presbytery to serve once again as a volunteer assistant pastor. (Actually, in each case the congregation pays a nominal salary which I return as a part of my pledge.)

These past years have been a time of real joy and enthusiasm for me. I have been warmly and loyally supported both by the pastors of the churches and by the congregations and sessions. I have been doing those things for which I was trained by my seminary. I am involved mostly with education and training of God's people for their work of ministry. I have concentrated on training church officers and church school teachers, teaching adult courses in Bible and theology, and limited preaching. All these areas are ones where my own strengths and abilities lie.

At the same time I have continued to serve an active role in the presbytery, on its committees, as a delegate to synod, and as a commissioner to the General Assembly. All this activity has been possible because the presbytery has supported and encouraged me in my rather peculiar position over the past years. Rather than raising objections to my doing things a little differently, the presbytery has smoothed the way and always made me feel a real part of its life and work.

Support is the word that best expresses the reaction I have found both within the local church and the presbytery. I am sure I would not have gone down this road with joy and enthusiasm if I had not had the support of pastors, session, congregation, and presbytery. I would encourage those in similar positions to give this same support when they have the opportunity. Support is also the role I see myself playing within the church. I am able to give support to the pastor, the session, the congregation, and the presbytery at the same time they are giving it to me.

My family has found this new role easier to live with than the previous one of the "pastor's family." There is a freedom for my wife to be herself and for my children to live out of the spotlight. It is similar to the freedom I have to say what I think within the church. In both cases we are on a free and honest basis with all those in the congregation. The major problem my family faces is the increased demands on my time these arrangements call for. Not only am I at work all day but many evenings I spend on church meetings. The one warning I have to give is that you must work hard to guard your time with your family.

One of the benefits I get from my non-church job, aside from the money to pay our bills, is having a concrete exposure to the daily problems of life and work that the members of the congregation also have. I find a real empathy for them in this very special identity I share with them. I have found that my sermons and my teaching of Bible and theology have been deeply and beneficially altered and shaped by my "other" job. In addition, I can speak openly and honestly about my daily experiences without exposing the private lives and problems of anyone in the congregation. All this leads me to the conviction that, for me, this is a better arrangement than I would ever be able to have working full time for a local congregation.

Finally, I think all who are interested in the future of the church and of our denomination ought to give much more serious thought to encouraging self-supporting clergy as a viable alternative. I hope the seminaries and the appropriate presbytery committees will be open to those who may feel that this is the path for them to take.

3.
ST. ANDREW'S TRIES A NEW APPROACH

Herman Page

For three years Herman Page combined being a half-time staff person at a community mental health center with the rectorate of St. Andrew's Episcopal Church, Liberal, Kansas. This history is adapted from an article in Crossroads, *the newsletter of the Rural Workers Fellowship.*

St. Andrew's Church, Liberal, Kansas, a small parish of around 200 communicants, is like many other small parishes in the Episcopal Church and faced with a problem common to many: how to meet rapidly increasing costs with a static or declining membership and income level. We tried to take a positive approach to this problem, which would continue the essential ministry of the church but to some degree take the money problem off our back.

By April of 1972, our financial crunch had become critical. Over the years, many more people had moved out of the parish than had come in, even with a large number of confirmations. Salary checks were consistently running behind. The parish was three months behind in payments to the diocese. Most of the vestry's concern and time went into the question, "How do we meet our bills?" Many smaller churches end up being almost completely survival-oriented, and we certainly were.

I proposed a plan that I find a part-time secular job. Initially the vestry was resistant, feeling that this would be a step backward for the parish. Yet they could find no other way to meet the problem. When work opened up in the local community mental health center, they reluctantly agreed to my taking the job, although having many questions in their minds. Here's how we did it:

1. I got an agreement of fixed hours from the mental health center, so that I would have a regular schedule there plus enough flexibility to allow me to meet real emergencies in the parish. I worked twenty hours a week, on Mondays, Tuesdays, and Wednesdays.

2. A vestry committee negotiated a "letter of agreement" between me and the vestry. We used the Diocese of Washington Clergy Association model and tried to define hours per week I would work and areas of primary responsibility. Also, I insisted that if this were going to work, we would need to have more lay responsibility, and some things I had been doing, mainly of an organizational nature, would have to be done (and properly could be done) by laity. We defined this in the letter of agreement. Salary, vacation, and other such matters were included.

3. We made provision for annual review and evaluation of my job performance by a committee of the vestry, not only as to how

I was doing in fulfilling the job description, but how the part-time work program was going and how it was affecting the parish. It was also helpful in that we could insist that clergy evaluation be on agreed-upon matters, not such extraneous things as the color of my socks or the type of car I drive. Clergy evaluation is always taking place, whether one likes it or not, and we found it good to provide for it in a constructive and definite manner.

4. I published my weekly schedule, showing time at the mental health center and time available for the parish. After three years, parishioners pretty well understood that I was just not available for routine matters on Tuesdays and Wednesdays, that questions about next Sunday's altar flowers would wait until Thursday. Once in a while a matter came up that could be dealt with by phone from the center between appointments, and occasionally when I had open time I could make an extra hospital call when needed. It sometimes meant making hospital visits in "civilian clothing" during the noon hour, or mailing the newsletters on the way home from work. Yet most lay people must do their church work in this same way.

Now, how did it work out after three years? The clergy evaluation was the most helpful part of the whole thing. People had a way of saying how they felt I had done my work and making suggestions for improvement. I could also express my feelings about how the vestry and other laity were doing what they agreed to.

Second, we now have more lay responsibility. Under the letter of agreement, the laity were totally responsible for buildings and grounds work, for organizing the choir, layreaders, church school, and youth work. I worked with them on a consulting basis, making suggestions for operation, program, and training leaders. While this doesn't work with one hundred percent effectiveness, it has meant that there has been a lot less of the attitude of "wait for Father to organize it." In some areas I simply reminded them, "If you want it but don't take responsibility for it, it probably won't get done." Our laity have done much more to help run their own church.

Third, just about half my salary came from an outside source, and so the financial burden on the church was much less. In most small parishes, well over half the income must go in one way or another to support the priest. My earnings on the outside released funds to pay up back bills, to make physical improvements on the property, and even more important, to have money for programs. I didn't have to worry about where to find a few dollars for some Sunday School material or to rent a film for the Lenten dinner. We had money to do things. Less vestry time was spent on financial matters and much more on what the church should be doing.

Fourth, better use was made of my time. Our parish is not unusual in that there were not enough demands on my time to keep me fully employed and occupied. There was not that much counselling, not that much demand for program. Many clergy in small churches spend time dreaming up programs which few people want, or get involved in all sorts of civic duties, in order to keep busy.

Obviously such a program has limitations. Let me suggest a few:

A. I don't think part-time secular work would be good in a parish this size when a priest first arrives. Fortunately, I had several years of full-time church work in order to get to know people and to get things done. Now I did not have time for the amount of "get acquainted" visiting that I feel is needed when a priest first goes to a church. If such a program is begun for a parish, probably the priest needs a period of full-time church work to let him get to know his parishioners.

B. There is less time for work in the diocese. Clergy of small churches are often asked to work on such things as youth camps and program commissions because they have more time. Part-time secular work makes this harder.

C. There was less time for ecumenical and community activities. I had been interested in ecumenical matters, and while on a full-time basis pushed a number of them. Since I quit pushing due to lack of time, many no longer take place. In a sense, this was a loss to the community and to the churches.

D. There was time pressure. I had to be much more careful about using my time well, to keep it scheduled, to use church time for church work, and to get things done on time. I used to find it easy to dribble time away on less important things, since there was time available. Now I had to try to make each day count for more. There was the problem of coming home after eight hours on the job, being drained and tired, and then facing a church meeting. Yet this was what many of our laity faced every time we clergy called a midweek evening meeting. I know now how it feels to leave work at 5:00 p.m. and go to junior choir practice; yet this is what our choir director did every Wednesday afternoon. I am thus much more sympathetic to lay people's feelings about unnecessary meetings and wanting to end things and go home.

In evaluating our program of part-time clergy secular work after three years, I can see no harm to the parish. All necessary work has been done: services held, confirmation classes taught, sick visited, dead buried, people counselled, new people welcomed, organizations operating, money coming in. If anything, the church is stronger from the point of view of increased lay responsibility and a stronger financial basis. My time is being better spent, and I am using more time for things I have been specifically trained to do. We have had limitations in the program. However, I thoroughly commend such an approach as *a* constructive way to maintain the mission and work of the church through missions or smaller parishes in our smaller communities.

4.
THE HIDDEN PRIESTHOOD

Harry A. Woggon

Father Woggon is Director of the Comprehensive Alcoholism Program, Blue Ridge Community Mental Health Center, and Honorary Assistant, St. Mary's Episcopal Church, Asheville, North Carolina.

Various styles of ministry are needed in our ever-changing age. There is a definite place for that open generalist, the parish rector. There is an equally definite place for a diversity of specialists who may often work hiddenly. All Christians, priests and people equally, are called to minister to the world on behalf of Christ, to be his hands and mouth and body, in whatever they do. That which draws men towards wholeness and peace is the work of the Holy Spirit. Invidious are the distinctions of first and second class, regular and irregular, full-time and part-time. Each style of ministry will be judged by the effectiveness with which the person has used the talents given him.

What shall we say of this ministry, this priesthood of all believers, as described in the New Testament, revived at the Reformation, and blossoming forth again in our own age? The vocation of the Christian, clergy and layfolk equally, is to be hidden and open at once; to be hid with Christ and God and deeply involved in the world; to move both in and out, as the natural rhythm of the heartbeat. It is, in short, a life and ministry that is "both/and," not "either/or."

For seven years the ministry was my full-time occupation, as curate, college chaplain, pastor of a small congregation, and school chaplain. But since then, I have served as a functional rather than an occupational priest. During the week I work for Buncombe County, North Carolina, where I am the Director of the Comprehensive Alcoholism Program of the Blue Ridge Community Mental Health Center. On Sundays I work as a diocesan supply priest and am attached officially but without pay to St. Mary's Church, Asheville, where my family is active.

The linking of a secular position and a church assignment is not always easy. When I moved to Asheville, I had hoped to be able to secure a funded but part-time church position to link with my new mental health position. None of the parishes which had expressed an interest in a part-time assistant were able to fund the position. Because I value a clear and conscious link with the institutional church, I have always sought to be attached officially, even if without pay, to a parish church.

In the first town to which I came to work for the department of mental health at a community clinic, my family and I were warmly welcomed at the only parish in the entire county, a small and ancient establishment. The rector, a man of great depth, strengths, and long residence, was most supportive from the beginning. He was not threatened by having another priest move into the parish, and he provided me with the designation of honorary assistant, with the privilege of leading worship on request and assisting whenever I was at home.

For over a year I was in sort of limbo, not exactly in nor yet quite out, being canonically resident in one diocese but physically resident in the neighboring one. While licensed to celebrate and preach in both dioceses, it was not clear where to place me and, as a result, I was on no mailing lists for conferences, meetings, etc. When the point was clearly made that while I might not be able to attend any of the meetings, I appreciated being invited as a sign of my regular standing as a priest, this problem cleared up.

After a year I took a position with Broughton Hospital, a large public psychiatric hospital in the foothills of North Carolina. For two years I worked as administrator/social worker/therapist at the alcohol unit of this institution. Three Sundays and one evening a month I functioned as vicar of Galloway Memorial Chapel, Elkin, North Carolina, a tiny mission whose regular Sunday congregation is fifteen to twenty persons. Either of these two positions alone would have been frustrating and depressing, but together they offered a fine balance and provided a richness unavailable in either by itself. The main disadvantage of this plan was that I lived in one town, worked in another, and had a church in a third place. This meant an hour's drive to work, in one direction, and a half-hour drive to church, in another direction. One of the attractions of coming to Asheville was to consolidate work, church, and home in the same community.

I arrived at this style of ministry by "push" and "pull." I was pulled toward the expression of priesthood in new forms. I was also pushed into this role because no suitable church positions were available when I needed to move. May not this be the unpredictable power of the Holy Spirit as well?

Unlike several of the men with whom I have worked (who have abandoned the ministry), I continued to regard myself as a priest. In conversation, these men who "used to be" ministers, would approach the subject obliquely. Quietly, one would half slip and say, "When I was in seminary . . ." After inquiry, it emerged that he had served various pulpits but lost faith, while another would admit that he was unhappy with the parish life of his denomination. They used to be ministers, but now were social workers or vocational rehabilitation workers, etc.

One day one of the ward personnel said that a patient was concerned about guilt and wanted to see the chaplain. As the chaplain happened to be away, she said to me, "You used to be a minister; why don't you see her?" I replied, "I still am," and then proceeded to see the girl. On another occasion, during an initial interview the patient paused and said, "I've told you more than I ever told my preacher." I said something about there being preachers and preachers, but smiled secretly. Once in a group therapy session, when one of the patients presented a very popular but confused notion of guilt, forgiveness, and a cruel god, and after my co-therapist had set me up for it, I spoke briefly about a loving God, free grace, and peace. Then I stopped with the words, "I had better stop; I'm changing roles." They all said "No! That was beautiful; we should ordain you." They were all amazed when the other therapist pointed out that I was already ordained.

Three years later, in another group, one lady with whom I had worked closely and who had just returned from a brief in-patient stay, blurted out in the middle of the group, "Did you know that Mr. Woggon was a priest? The nurse at the hospital said you give good sermons. I have been wondering how you can mix psychology and religion." The rest of the group affirmed and supported me in my conviction that religion and psychology can be quite naturally linked. On several occasions I have met people who normally knew me through the hospital or the mental health center. If I am wearing a collar or vested in church, there is an immediate double-take. And once at a cocktail party a secretary dropped her drink when I came in. The both/and approach has to be explained again and again. I am regarded by one of my superiors as the "Christian in residence." At the hospital I was sometimes thought of as the social worker, period; not as a priest who served as a social worker. In fact, in the beginning, it was made clear that any pastoral or priestly functions, per se, were the prerogative of one of the chaplains. In order to insure the freedom of the other staff members, I kept these distinctions intact. However, after being accepted as a staff member who was not a threat to others, I was able quietly to speak and act more openly in the name of the Lord. Yet even without the Divine Name being spoken, the loving care of persons in every aspect of the job is a valid Christian priesthood, after the order of Creation, as well as that of Melchizedek.

A very important point was made by the physician who was originally instrumental in my securing a position with the department of mental health. When I had an opportunity to thank him for his support these past several years, he replied that while he could open the door for me, he would not have been able to support me had I not been able to do suitable clinical work. Indeed, I was considered for my present position because of my work at the hospital, and only secondarily because of my work as a priest.

When you work for the state, own your own home, pay your own pension premiums, and wear civilian clothes (the collar only on Sundays and never at the office), you become more and more like the generality of men. No longer are you set apart or given the highest seat. The daily pressures of other men become yours as well. There is a certain freedom in work on a regular basis, but there are also the restrictions that you must be there and only have an hour off for lunch. With petty time and vacation days to be calculated and reported, the long lunch hour or afternoon off are more carefully chosen than in the more general freedom, and bind, of the twenty-four-hour, seven-day a week parish life. Working as a mental health specialist, whether at a community mental health center or in a large public psychiatric hospital, your only tool is yourself. There are no props of ancient clerical status to hide behind. You are accepted or rejected on your performance and your personal effectiveness. (This may also be true in the parish, but not so obviously.)

In parish life much can be excused as eccentricities of the clergy; in secular life fewer such allowances are made. In this work, more so than in the parish, I am forced to look at myself and examine how I come across to patients and staff. If you are trying to help others to be in touch with their feelings and to live at peace with them, you have to be in touch and at peace with your own. This ongoing process, painful at times, of facing yourself honestly and acknowledging the shadows, enables you to become more aware of both strengths and weaknesses. As you become more and more aware of yourself, you are able to modify your behavior and thereby grow stronger. In this process the inner resources you have are activated. You may truly be rooted and grounded in the Lord and not in the institutional church or the Book of Common Prayer or the cassock and collar.

In our dreams, if we are aware of them, we can see our unconscious selves working out personal problems we may only be partly aware of in our conscious selves. When I was first taking up this form of ministry, I had several recurring dreams that are significant and fairly easily interpreted. In the dream I am in the sacristy getting ready for the service, the congregation is waiting, and the organist is playing. I am trying to get dressed and I have every vestment but the right one; I search frantically for the appropriate vestment. Or I am in the back of the church just as the procession is to begin. I have the proper book but as I flip the pages I can't find the right one. The prelude is played again and again, but I am unable to give the signal to begin, as I cannot find the page.

What is the right page and appropriate vestment for the self-supporting minister? We discover that it is neither cassock nor coat, collar nor tie, open nor hidden, but rather both/and. Each in his own person becomes a bridge over troubled waters to make this possible for himself, and perhaps for others who would like to try this style and form of ministry.

If we are to be this bridge, we must be firmly rooted. We are also called upon to be the outward and visible sign of God. This is only possible if the essential priestly work of prayer and meditation continues. This may be done publicly and physically at the altar in the parish church building on Sundays. It may equally be done privately and spiritually (after the manner of Pierre Teilhard de Chardin on the steppes of Asia) at the altar of the world, in the car en route to work at sunrise each day. This daily, conscious offering of work and joy and pain and suffering and personal intercession, in the midst of an unseen eternal congregation, is at least as fulfilling as the weekly celebration, in the midst of a seen, temporal congregation.

During the hour's drive to work, the entire Eucharist is offered. From time to time the mind wanders and the needs of driving demand attention. But these are no different from the distractions that present themselves in an hour's meditation, say, in a perfectly

appointed monastic chapel. This inward movement at the
beginning of day is most essential for movement outward the rest
of the day.

This is a ministry of presence and power to people in need of
wholeness and health — people who would seldom come to the
parish church or any church, people with whom you work who
are only vaguely aware of God. This is a ministry broad and deep,
that is not content with easy dichotomies of either/or but rather
rejoices in being both hidden and open at once, functional as well
as occupational, in the service of the Lord God and all creation.

5.
STARTING WITH MOONLIGHTING

Eugene S. Patton

*Eugene Patton is Director of Media Services at
Chestnut Hill Academy, a private school for boys, and
serves St. Thomas Episcopal Church in Morgantown,
Pennsylvania.*

One of the side effects of the worker ministry is that not all
things can be done in time or in depth. This is written, therefore,
with much haste.

I began moonlighting in September, 1971. Before that,
beginning in June, 1966, I had been serving two tiny parishes
only four miles apart, in two different dioceses. Each parish was
receiving aid from its diocese. In the fall of 1969, one diocese
decided its priority lay with college ministry rather than with a
place that had not been self-supporting for generations.

That threw me into a crisis, because the other diocese, while
willing to continue its aid, could not be expected to pick up the
additional tab. There were three choices: 1) I could be called to
a place that could afford me. This seemed unlikely, because I had

entered the priesthood at the age of forty-two, had served small parishes, and no cathedral had sought me out to be dean. In fact, I had not received a call from *any* parish, large or small, so how could I expect one now? 2) I could leave the active ministry and move to where I could find a secular job. 3) I could stay with one parish and get another job on the side.

I decided to stay in the ministry simply because I feel called to this, especially the parish ministry. After surveying the possibilities, I decided to go back to school and retool, choosing the general field of education because of its approximately 180 days a year rather than 250, specializing in educational media (audio-visuals). So in January of 1970, at the age of fifty, I began taking two courses a semester; in August, 1971, I received the degree of Master in Educational Media from Temple University.

During the spring of 1971 I sent out letters to seventy-five or eighty private schools and junior colleges (having found out that I was ineligible for public school unless I took several further education courses and did practice teaching). Only about half the schools bothered to answer, and those who did said "No," with one sterling exception. I went for an interview, sweated it out for another three or four weeks, and was hired!

My job was audio-visual coordinator at the Chestnut Hill Academy, a private school for boys near Philadelphia. At the end of the first year the head librarian retired, and I was offered the job. I accepted and that summer started at Drexel University, working towards a Master's in Library Science, which I hope to finish in 1976.

During the winter and spring of 1970-1971, prodded by diocesan headquarters, the vestry and I worked out a letter of agreement which was duly approved by the bishop. Rather than being based on so many days or hours spent in or for the parish, the new relationship is evaluated on the basis of how satisfied the vestry and parishioners are with the arrangement. This is good, because my job is forty-three miles from home, and my average week away from home is fifty to fifty-five hours. I receive no cash salary from the church, but the parish furnishes housing and utilities, keeps up the pension premium, gives me a $500 car allowance, and pays for the diocesan group life and major medical insurances.

We have one service on Sunday, and church school for adults and children. We have services on Ash Wednesday, Maundy Thursday, and Good Friday; often we will celebrate a Holy Day with communion in someone's house; and we have begun to make Eucharist at our parish dinners some four or five times a year.

In my secular job, where I have the fancy title of Director of Media Services, several of my colleagues look upon me as pastor. I hear confessions (informally), and from time to time I find myself in a counselling situation. I wear a clerical shirt three or four times a month, just to make sure that there is no mistake about my primary job. (That is what may seem strange: The great bulk of my time and energy are spent in my secular job, but I still think of myself primarily as a parish priest.)

I am not sure that my moonlighting has a great deal of effect on the parish. We are quite small (thirty-four households, ninety-six baptized members, a $10,000 budget), and not much activity goes on in the parish, compared with a larger place. I have always encouraged lay leadership and generally tried to do nothing that a lay person can do. We are blessed with a core of people who are willing to take responsibility and leadership and to get things done. If my moonlighting has any effect, it is constantly to remind the parish of its precarious position; the parish had not had a rector since 1906 until I came in 1966, and the economics being what they are, I am probably the last rector for a long, long time to come.

My situation is not one that I would recommend indiscriminately. Several things help to make it work for me. 1) When I began, all of my children were out of the house, either at college or married or living and working away. If there had been kids at home, I am not sure I would have had enough energy to go around. 2) I am not on a career ladder. When I entered seminary at age thirty-eight, I had had enough successes to help satisfy the craving to move up, up, and up. The craving is not bad, and I am not knocking it; it's just that I didn't find it operating for me after ordination. 3) I had been in the parish long enough for people to know me and to know pretty well what they were getting into. I am not sure this same arrangement would work with a priest coming in cold from the outside. Conversely, I am not sure I could make it work in another parish. From 1966 to 1970, I had enough time to make parish calls, get to know people, and learn the taboos and shibboleths. Now I am operating on the capital built up during those years. Starting from scratch again there would be no such capital. 4) Perhaps most important, my wife Nancy is my biggest support, morally, emotionally, and if need be, financially. Nancy is a librarian in two elementary schools nearby. This means that we can talk shop, which I find is a great blessing. Also, her income made it needless for me to panic when the crunch came; we could plot out the future free from the fear that must clutch the hearts of many clergy families with only one income when faced with a job loss.

Life is not all roses, of course. Like most clergymen, I face the dilemma of not enough time for either family or parish. I look forward wistfully to the first summer with no school, both so that I can get some rest, and also that I can build up the operating capital again. In general, however, for me and for the parish, moonlighting seems to work.

6.
LINKS AND MERGINGS OF INTEREST

George E. McCullogh

Mr. McCullogh is an Industrial Consultant and Rector of St. Stephen's Episcopal Church, Hamburg, Michigan.

In the mid-1950's my secular work and my church interests began to merge. I was manager of manufacturing for the Chemical Development Department of the General Electric Company. The department was learning how to manufacture commercially a polymer recently discovered in the laboratory. It soon became apparent that we would also need to know how to manage both the people and the business more effectively if we were to become commercially competitive with the large chemical companies with already-established polymer businesses.

At this time my family and I were members of St. Stephen's Church, Pittsfield, Massachusetts. The rector, Fr. Malcolm Eckel, had been an accountant before he embarked on his clerical career. For a time I served as treasurer of the parish. We found that our interests in the development of people and organizations were well aligned. Over a four year span, we came to agree that, with respect to human relations, an organization of people, whether religious or secular, has identical characteristics. The needs of the people involved were: 1) to be free to make their own decisions as to their personal actions, and 2) to have the necessary information, education, and skills to assure that these decisions would work out to the advantage of all concerned. Both St. Stephen's Church and the commercial polymer business prospered in their respective fields.

Later on, I moved to southern Indiana to build and manage a commercial plant for the manufacture of the new polymeric material. My interest in the development of persons and organizations was aroused when I found myself a member of a 113-year-old mission whose young vicar was determined to make all decisions by himself regarding the function of the church. When I suggested that I would like to help in developing the mission, he, in effect, patted my head and told me that I just did not understand the church business.

Several years later, finding that most commercial management philosophy was to let each manager "do his own thing" rather than to utilize technically proven precepts, I seized on an opportunity to join the Institute for Social Research at the University of Michigan. While living in Ann Arbor, I was able to teach management in the field and to participate in research. Within a few years, I was instrumental in forming my own consulting firm to practice management development full time.

Full time, I should say, was an overstatement, for as soon as I arrived in Michigan, I found the Diocesan School of Theology. Bishop Richard Emrich was sympathetic to my call, had me enroll in the school, and later accepted me as a candidate for Holy Orders.

Under the direction of the Rev. R. H. Whitaker, director of the school, and the Rev. Colin Campbell, Jr., rector of St. Clare of Assissi, Ann Arbor, at that time, I either attended classes or interned Friday evenings, Saturdays, Sundays, and Monday evenings for four years. I "vacationed" at the Graduate School of Theology at the University of the South, Sewanee, Tennessee. These summers were invaluable experiences; I developed a more spiritual regimen and discovered that the School of Theology in Detroit had prepared me so that I could be competitive with seminary graduates. Bishop H. Coleman McGehee ordained me to the diaconate in December, 1971, and the priesthood in December, 1973.

While I was obtaining religious training, I was also learning the art of consulting. It is one thing, I found, to manage a plant where people want to learn, want to make decisions, and want to use all the data they can absorb in order to be independent. It is another to attempt to convince the skeptical, traditional manager that these fine things can really happen.

The consultant is a person from outside the group who is expected to know the industry and to be able to advise in its operation. He is different from the client organization manager. The self-supporting clergyman is "different" too. It is very difficult for him to be seen as part of the group by the stipendiary clergy, and to some extent this applies to his wife and children. In such matters as scheduling meetings, showing interest in pursuing comparisons of the secular and religious worlds, and accepting the legitimacy of secular vocations, the conventional brothers seldom consider the position of non-stipendiary men, whom they regard as "part-time" clergy.

I was most fortunate to be considered for a vacant cure in a parish established in 1844 and still functioning in the original building. This parish of some forty families had never in current memory been able to support a full-time stipendiary clergyman, nor had it ever been financially dependent on the diocese. In my interviews with the vestry and in speaking to the congregation, I emphasized that I had a full-time secular job and that I would be pleased to be their rector on the basis that I would be priest, teacher, counsellor, and member of the congregation to whatever extent time permitted. However, I would not be "in charge" of operations nor responsible for the routine things normally associated with the parish priest. Crises, yes! Routine, no! Ninety percent of the congregation accepted these conditions, and I became rector. That vote, by the way, in October, 1973, was the last official vote taken by the vestry or parish meeting at St. Stephen's. All decisions since then have been made by obtaining a consensus.

My religious job and my secular job are wonderfully congruent; only the settings and the language are different. The objectives in both are to create an environment in which people are able to become fulfilled persons, capable through knowledge, training, and experience to transmit God's love for their fellow men in the warmth, support, and appreciation of God's love.

Being ordained, having the training and experience of preparation for ordination, and being responsible without temporal authority for a growing congregation, has, I believe, materially improved my functioning as a counsellor to large industrial plants. I have learned, experientially, that I must operate without controlling and evaluating others, but rather with a deep sense of empathy for people in their own unique situations.

Plant managers who are able to be responsive to impersonal corporate needs, and at the same time be responsive to the very personal needs of their people, have proven to be the most successful leaders. It must be recognized that to be of help in the business world requires a great deal of knowledge and competence in the technology of the industry and the economic situation, and the ability to extend God's love to his people. This is a difficult mission that requires much support and guidance from the Spirit. Providing this support is my call, both in the church and in the secular world.

A tentmaker has a fruitful area to cultivate. It requires time that it is difficult to come by. It requires flying in the face of customs that are well established. It requires faith in the power of the Spirit and patience in large measure, knowing that the Lord works in his own time and his own ways. Finally, it requires the support, warmth, and fellowship from family, superiors, and friends who believe that this vocation is worthwhile.

7.
BLUER SKY AND GREENER GRASS

Frances S. Schwannecke

Fran Schwannecke is semi-retired as head of a leasing-rental business in Saginaw, Michigan, and a perpetual deacon ministering to the senior citizenry of five area Episcopal churches and the larger Saginaw community, out of St. John's Parish. She was originally trained as an accountant.

Over two years ago I was ordained to the diaconate in the Protestant Episcopal Church in the United States of America. At that time the sky looked bluer and the grass greener as I contemplated the glorious years ahead serving our Lord in the capacity of deacon. As the years have passed since, I have never gotten over the wonder of how I, most inadequate and certainly ill-prepared at the time, could be chosen by our Lord for this position.

Before my husband's death twelve years ago, he and I were operating a leasing-rental business, called Ed's Rental Service, in Saginaw, Michigan. We founded it in 1945, the first in our area, and worked hard as a team both to acquire equipment and to educate people to use it. After my husband's death, my son Tom, who had entered the business, and I made a pact to strive towards making this rental service the best in Michigan. So we worked seven days and most nights every week, planning, studying, and convincing the people of Saginaw of the advantages of renting needed equipment.

The rental industry during those years was growing by leaps and bounds. Many rental services over the country were owned and operated by couples, and they soon became known as "ma and pa" businesses. Many of the "pas" died young, as did my husband, and I discovered, to my amazement, how competent and knowledgeable women became when they were forced to run their own businesses. It was probably then that the first seeds of my belief in the capability and equality of women were implanted.

A new widow who has experienced a happy life with her partner, as I did, feels completely lost and alone. Her first need is to know that God *is*, that she is his child, and that he loves and cares and comforts. By the grace of God I believe this, and I desired to study the Scriptures for better understanding and enlightenment. That January the Episcopal School of Theology of the Diocese of Michigan opened classes in Saginaw, and I was offered the opportunity to attend.

A whole new world opened up for me, and I marveled. I did not begin my studies with the idea of becoming ordained. I was just hungry at the time and needed to be fed. I was a student in the school for five years before any idea of ordination entered my mind. For some time I had been visiting shut-ins at home and in rest homes, and the deplorable conditions and hopelessness of the patients made me fighting mad. I suddenly realized I could serve and fight for them better as a deacon. I hesitated making known my desires, not believing a businesswoman of long standing could possibly have enough to offer in the religious or devotional life.

God had always been real in my life, or so I thought. I had been superintendent of the Sunday school, our children were brought up in the church, my husband served at the altar, but God had never ridden in the front seat with me. I had never really believed that prayers are always answered, but in *his* way, not mine. I had never truly understood the joy of being a child of God, believing all the promises Christ has given to each of us. But God's presence had now become so real that I seemed to feel his hands on my shoulders — pushing, pulling, strengthening, picking me up and brushing me off when I fell. Still, studying and remembering were hard for me, and many times I felt like quitting.

During a total of eight years study, my son Tom and I were working hard long hours building up the business. Over our door hung a sign placed there years ago by my husband, which read, "Through this door pass the best people on earth, our customers." I had read this hundreds of times but, after a few years of theological study, the statement came to have special meaning, and we really began to treat our customers in a friendlier, more caring way. Our services sprang into new focus. Customers responded, and our rental shop became a well-known and respected business in the area. We moved to a new location, built another and larger store, and expanded into renting contractors' equipment.

You recall that old saying, "The customer is always right." Perhaps our belief did not go quite that far, but we now gave him the benefit of the doubt. A Christian love began to creep into our business. Minority persons, both black and Chicano, began appearing and reappearing in our shop, for they found a fair deal there. We prospered, our business doubled, then tripled; and I know it to be directly due to the teachings of our Lord which were being poured into my mind and soul, and which I, in turn, attempted to pour out to my son and our employees.

Also, I learned from my customers that the true ministry of anyone, both clergy and lay, is in daily contacts with any person one meets or does business with. Customers began to stick their heads in my door and say, "Fran, got a minute?" and then proceed to relate to me their problems, whether a particularly trying situation with mate, relative, child, or work.

These were difficult but tremendously challenging years, which climaxed in my ordination to the diaconate in April of 1973. On my ordination night, each member of my family was caught up in the spirit of the momentous and joyous occasion, and I believe the vows I made that night were silently and humbly voiced by each of them.

My parish, St. John's, is an urban church situated in the heart of a business district. We number about 450 families, totalling about 1,250 parishioners. We have a rector, an associate, a rector emeritus, and myself, a deacon. I was ordained particularly to work with and serve the elderly and, as there are five Episcopal parishes in the immediate area, my work includes, as much as possible, the elderly in these parishes also.

Most of the members of our families have lived in Saginaw all their lives, and it is always gratifying to hear someone say when I am calling, "Oh, I knew your husband. I rented tools from him when he first opened." Or, "I used to buy coal from your grand-father." Immediately a rapport is formed; we find much to talk about, and their need of God, his church, or his clergy is much more easily expressed. These contacts are quite rewarding, for these people relate to their friends and, when I visit any of them, the door is open, the stage is set, and we have a companionable visit with good results.

There are three ministries of a deacon: 1) the ministry of liturgy; 2) the ministry of the word; 3) the ministry of service. To me, each one has proved to be exciting, challenging, gratifying, exasperating, rewarding, surprising, and joyful. My rector recognizes these three functions of the deacon and allows and encourages my work and service to the fullest extent in all three.

There has been total acceptance from parishioners. I remember one canonical exam which I failed — an oral in history. (Imagine an old gal like me even attempting this!) It was humiliating to come back and tell of my failure; but, during the two months of study for another try, I was glad it happened, for the congregation's wonderful support and concern and prayer strengthened me and, also, brought us closer together. That's what it's all about, isn't it?

My motto for the oldsters became "Faith, fight, and fun!"

Faith. I remember one suffering and feeble old lady who showed me a hymn she had sung as a girl, and then offered to sing it for me. She raised her trembling voice and tenderly sang the words: "My Savior, God to Thee, how great art Thou, how great Thou art." I was forced to turn to the window blinking rapidly. Here was faith in the highest degree, and the presence of the living Lord was very near.

Fight. There was a delightful old woman from New England whose favorite saying was "Hell's bells and oyster shells." One night, after a long fight, when she was failing fast, she opened her eyes and whispered, "Hell's bells and oyster shells." And I whispered back, "Yes, and his everlasting arms." She tried to smile, and died before morning. There was courage, and she had that faith and fight I believe in.

Fun. One of my duties is taking taped sermons to shut-ins. One afternoon, while listening to the tapes, my ninety-year-old lady, who was sipping a glass of what appeared to be wine, insisted I join her and have one too. I took a good swallow, coughed, choked, and almost strangled, while she innocently remarked, "Oh, you don't like Four Roses?"

Truly, the ministry of the tentmaker, female or male, priest or deacon, is a needed and necessary ministry. I know every parish would be enriched and enhanced through this ministry. I have found fulfillment and my heart is filled with gratitude: gratitude to God for choosing and preparing and guiding me; gratitude to my bishop for understanding and supporting my call and desire; gratitude to my rector for his acceptance and support.

8.
A COMPLEMENTARY MINISTRY

William L. Mengebier

Dr. Mengebier is Chairman of the Department of Biology of Bridgewater College in Virginia and vicar of a small parish at the foot of the Blue Ridge Mountains.

For the past twenty-eight years I have been a practicing scientist involved with teaching, research, and administration. Within the scope of my experience, I can be termed successful, having received awards from my peers and from those for whom I have worked. Above all, I am as thrilled with my everyday interactions, personal and intellectual, as I was the first day I entered a classroom. I am happy in what I do.

For the past eight years, I have been an ordained priest of the Episcopal Church. During that time I have served as vicar of a small parish in a beautiful valley at the foot of the Blue Ridge Mountains with a joy and excitement that is truly beyond expression, I consider myself a fortunate individual.

Obviously, the assumption of Holy Orders by a scientist would be expected to raise questions from both environments in which I work, and it has. The greatest criticism has come from my scientific friends, who in the main have been kind but concerned. To a lesser degree, laity and clergy have expressed reservations both as to my theological background (I read for Orders) and the tentmaker concept itself. From both sides, I have received a few critical comments that have hurt, ranging from the scientist who questioned my mental state to the clergyman who spoke pointedly of my ego trips. Yet the overall reaction from both groups has been support, acceptance, and interest, with the ever-present question, "How did it happen?"

Actually, when it happened, two facets of the experience became totally bound together. First, I found the priesthood by the call of mental, intellectual, and even physical forces beyond my belief and understanding. Second, my call to minister in its theological sense was involved with the community of college life within which I worked as a scientist. In addition to these parameters of my call, there has grown the need for an altar in order to fulfill totally my personal need in the priesthood.

To some, the idea of being a weekend or emergency vicar and a member of an academic organization may seem to be a compartmentalization of intellect and belief. This has not happened in my case, insofar as I am aware. The rural atmosphere of both my college and my parish church eliminates a possible dichotomy of atmosphere which could become a problem. On the other hand, academic structure, as compared with a mountain mission social structure, would not seem to lend itself to similar experiences. Yet this is exactly what I have found. People at all levels of age and experience do feel the need for being recognized, for being ministered to, and for being made aware of their worth. Never let us forget that it is the college student, twisted and torn by conflicting disciplines and ideologies, who is less likely than almost anyone else to recognize the church as having any counsel of value.

The role of the tentmaker or worker priest within the college community is to "be there." In order to be there, he must be recognized for his own academic credentials, or else he becomes a "hanger on" with no real slot into which the student can peg him. The student must recognize the secular before he will see the ordained. The student will judge the secular before he will seek out the ordained. It is within this context that a minister may function with a degree of acceptance by the college community.

I feel that this is a true reflection of what the ministry has always been about. The tendency to see one's priestly functions as taking place only within the confines of a collar or a church building can effectively block out the real world, and our priest-hood is concerned with reality. All too often the student or the faculty member is blocked from peace of mind by a real or imagined threat from what he or she thinks the church is. It does no good to scoff at some of these images; the point is that the setting of this imagery keeps people from touching, understanding, and forgiveness. For those who seek comfort, the faculty office contains an individual they know in a surrounding they know, and they do come — many more than is perhaps realized. The process of recognition and acceptance of the ordained within this position of the secular world is a slow one. There must never be the slightest hint that ordination in any way acts to censor or restrict the teaching of an academic discipline. Conversely, there must never be the slightest hint that the ordination may be bent to meet the demands of secularity. The college community may laugh at the meaning of ordination but will damn you if you distort that meaning.

These comments in no way presume that all parish priests are out of touch with reality because they have no secular profession. The majority of priests I know are extremely realistic, but the fact remains that by chance or design there are certain secular niches from which the clergyman, if not barred, is at least discouraged from entering. I work in one of these niches.

My work as a parish priest has been complemented by my secular position, just as I feel my secular position has been confirmed by my parish role. As I mentioned earlier, the full expression of priesthood requires an altar, and I truly cannot see myself as a priest without the possibility of regularly celebrating the Holy Eucharist. In my case, the assignment by my bishop to parish work has not only enabled me to perform the liturgical duties that all priests should engage in, but it has also given me the opportunity to reconcile differences in ideas, needs, potentials, and even fears from two wholly diverse cultures into one concept of man seeking a relationship with the Christ and peace with his God. Perhaps this acceptance and appreciation of the universal loneliness and seeking of all people, regardless of economic or intellectual status, can be arrived at without being a worker priest, but in my own case I doubt it. In the beginning of my ministry, I had fears of role playing, of trying to prove my priesthood in my secularity and my secular profession in my priesthood. This has passed, and the two have blended into what is for me a continuum. To be sure, there are frustrations, many of them. The lack of everyday pastoral care that is the lot of my parish, my inability to reach every hospital bed in time, the cancellation of a wedding to attend a scientific meeting at which I am to present a paper, or the cancellation of the paper to perform a wedding: — these are part and parcel of the continuum.

I suppose that the ultimate question every worker priest must both ask and answer is, "Would you give up the secular job you hold for a full-time ministry?" Frankly, I do not know whether there is an answer that applies to everyone; I do not know the answer insofar as I am concerned. My own situation I have described many times as being the best of two worlds, although I do not see them as separate, but as two expressions of a single theme. The beginning of each school year is as challenging to me as it was the first time I entered a classroom. The preaching of the Gospel is a new experience for me every time I step into the pulpit. This way of life which has been granted to me is at present indivisible. Perhaps the time will come when I will move into a full-time expression of my priesthood within the parish situation; this is a possibility, and opportunities have been offered me. Yet within this secular community in which I achieve, I sense the ever-present needs of those young people in whom the future of this small planet of ours both resides and depends. For them, the organized church and all that is associated with it, including the clergy, has become if not irrelevant, then of minor influence. Why this is I cannot presume to say, and though this attitude generally changes as the years go by, during the college years it certainly dominates the decision-making processes of student life. But the student does hope and fear, the student does have doubt and certainty, the student does have joy and sorrow, and it is here that I minister.

9.
NUCLEAR STUDIES AND PARISH MINISTRY

William G. Pollard, Ph.D.

Dr. Pollard is Executive Director, Oak Ridge Associated Universities, and priest associate, St. Stephen's Episcopal Church, Oak Ridge, Tennessee.

In 1947 I was appointed Executive Director of the recently formed Oak Ridge Associated Universities (then called Oak Ridge Institute of Nuclear Studies). I was at the time professor of physics at the University of Tennessee. We lived in Knoxville, and my wife and I and four young sons went to St. John's Church there. Although I had been confirmed in the church, I had left it in my late teens and did not return until my marriage in 1932. Since then I had not become very active or interested in the church other than Sunday attendance. After my appointment, we obtained housing in Oak Ridge and moved into the house where we still live, after Christmas in 1947.

At that time there were no church buildings, other than an Army chapel, in the city, which was then entirely government owned. A small but very enthusiastic Episcopal congregation had been formed as a mission and was holding services in the Oak Ridge High School gymnasium. I rapidly became more and more involved and became successively chairman of a building fund drive, member of the vestry, superintendent of the church school, and layreader. By then we had become a parish and called the Rev. Robert F. McGregor as our rector. In 1949 we purchased land from the government, and our church building was completed in 1951. In this period the Oak Ridge Associated Universities, which I headed, had become a contractor of the new Atomic Energy Commission and had grown from one employee (myself) to nearly two hundred. It was a very exciting period both in the parish and in ORAU.

In the church school I had begun a study of the collects for a sermonette at the opening children's service. In this way I had become fascinated with liturgics and also discovered an immense satisfaction in leading worship, which later led to my layreader's license. This, combined with the impact on me of an ordination sermon, led to a decision that I wanted to study theology in depth. The best way to do this was organized preparation under the canons for the priesthood, since at that time there was no regular perpetual diaconate canon. Father McGregor arranged a conference with the bishop, and he with the chairman of the board of examining chaplains. A course of study was laid out with the recommended texts, and Father McGregor agreed to supervise my studies with regular monthly meetings. Late in 1949 I was admitted as a postulant for Holy Orders.

We began my studies with the Old Testament, which I found fascinating and so exciting that I did not mind the very considerable amount of time required. The main text we used was R. H. Pfeiffer's *Introduction to the Old Testament.* One discovery I made in the course of this study was the Early Source of Samuel, which so intrigued me that, after ordination, I turned back to this topic in greater detail, met Dr. Pfeiffer, and collaborated with him in publishing his translation with my commentary as *The Hebrew Illiad* (Harper & Row 1957). During my diaconate, Daniel Lang of *The New Yorker* spent ten days with me in Oak Ridge and wrote a profile, "A Deacon in Oak Ridge," which was published in the February 6, 1954, issue of the magazine. I was priested in mid-1954.

I served as priest associate in St. Stephen's until 1957 when, at the request of the bishop, I took over St. Francis's, Norris, for a year and a half as priest-in-charge during a vacancy. This meant a very demanding schedule, with all of Sunday in Norris every week plus about three evenings a week for meetings of the mission council and other organizations and pastoral work. I greatly enjoyed having the sole responsibility for this cure, however, and found great personal satisfaction from the intimacy of the relations of the priest with his people. During the last six months, a deacon was assigned full time by the diocese, and as soon as he was priested, I returned to St. Stephen's as priest associate.

A year later the rector and vestry of St. Stephen's decided to sponsor the formation of a parochial mission in the nearby city of

Clinton, and I agreed to take on that task. We started Sunday evenings in the municipal recreation building. In the spring of 1960 a residential property in a good location came up for sale, and St. Stephen's purchased it. By 1962 St. Alban's had grown to the point that we decided to build an adjacent chapel. I had the immense satisfaction of designing this building from scratch with all its appointments. This was done with the help of Canon Edward West of New York and Father Kurt Junker of Tulsa, together with a visit I had made to the Church of St. Severin in Paris while attending an international scientific conference there. The result was a real gem with a number of liturgically significant features.

By 1964 the burden of my secular employment, combined with being priest-in-charge at St. Alban's, was beginning to tell on me. Another priest was called to take over St. Alban's, and I returned to the less demanding role of priest associate at St. Stephen's, and this has continued without interruption since then. For two-thirds of 1974 we were without a rector, and I took complete charge of the parish (but with considerable lay assistance in administration and pastoral care). This I had done on two previous occasions between rectors. My relation with our new rector is excellent and mutually supportive for the great benefit of our total ministry to the parish. Throughout this whole period, my parish has paid for me the minimum assessment of the Church Pension Fund and an expense allowance of twenty-five dollars per month. Mine has thus been a non-stipendiary ministry both as deacon and priest for twenty-three years.

Contrary to general belief, my scientific career had nothing to do with my pilgrimage into the priesthood. There was, however, a great deal of publicity following my first ordination in 1952, the result of which was tremendous pressure on me to speak on "Science and Religion." I was ill-prepared to do so at the time, but the unrelenting pressure forced me to think through the relationship between these two realities in my life. This required a great deal of intellectual and theological effort, which in time led to an invitation to give the Kellogg lectures at the Episcopal Theological School (later published by Scribners as *Chance and Providence* in 1957), the Paddock lectures at the General Theological Seminary (published in 1961 by the Seabury Press as

Physicist and Christian), and a special lectureship at the Claremont Colleges in California, which was published in 1967 as *Man on a Space Ship*. My most recent book is *Science and Faith — Twin Mysteries* in the Thomas Nelson Youth Forum Series.

In 1955 I was elected as the clerical trustee of the University of the South by my diocesan convention and held this position for some years. I was also made vice chairman of the Joint Commission of General Convention on the Peaceful Uses of Atomic Energy, which resulted in the gift of a nuclear research reactor to St. Paul's University in Tokyo. This project was approved by General Convention in Miami Beach in 1958 and carried to a successful conclusion in 1961. A nationwide effort through all dioceses of the Episcopal Church raised $300,000 for the purpose, and I negotiated and supervised (with much help from local experts) the contract between General Atomic and the Episcopal Church for the construction of a Triga reactor at the University's Institute for Nuclear Research at Yokosuka. I was a Deputy to General Convention in 1958 and 1961 and Chairman of the House of Deputies Committee on National and International Problems in 1964 and 1967.

It is evident that I have had a very rich and rewarding priesthood, which has been a source of great joy to me. I have a deep and lovely relationship with my whole parish maintained over many years of loving intimacy in Christ with numerous families. God has provided me with numerous and very diverse opportunities for sharing my faith with others, and I never cease to give him thanks for making this very special ministry possible for me, and to the Holy Spirit for steering me into such an unexpected and unsought turning point in my life a quarter of a century ago. I am confident that the nonstipendiary priesthood can be a potent force in the church today if it is embraced joyfully as a lifetime commitment, and I pray that God will put it into the hearts of many to offer themselves for this ministry.

10.
MINISTRY IN THE SPACE COMMUNITY

Carl Praktish

> *Carl Praktish, in his career with the National Aeronautic and Space Agency, has been involved in such manned spaceflight programs as the Apollo lunar landings, the Skylab earth orbital flights and the recent Apollo-Soyuz mission. He is a priest of the Episcopal Diocese of Virginia. His ministry is within the aerospace community, the clergy community, and the community at St. Patrick's, Georgetown, in Washington, D.C., where he is on staff.*

How do I select from all the thoughts that go tumbling through my mind when I take this moment to reflect on the worker ministry as I have experienced it? My criterion has been to select those that are more universal, in the hope that they may be of some value to others as they reflect upon their own vocation or seek further understanding of the worker ministry. It seems logical to comment on three commonly-asked questions:

1. How do you keep going? What really is the source of identity that keeps you functioning creatively at a time of conflicting role expectations about the ministry?

2. How do you handle the tensions between your vocation and your job? How do you integrate two different worlds? How does your job affect your theology?

3. What are the options open to you for ministry?

The first question comes up in two ways. First there are those who think of the ministry as an institutional role. For instance, clergy who have entered the worker ministry from a full-time parochial position often have a grief process to work through, for there is a loss of an old role model that gave their work legitimacy: the parish priest. Clergy who have come into the worker ministry as part of their career development are also seeking a model which will assure them a sense of legitimacy, recognition, and support from the church.

Another group which raises this question also gives a clue to the answer. One corporate president, who by all secular standards "had made it," said in a private moment that he had seen the crucifixion, but never the resurrection, in his life. There was no doubt in his mind that the world ran by its own laws. Man struggled in anxiety for a lonely existence. Competition and manipulation, rather than any form of love, were the norms for relationship. Promethean people view the world in mechanistic terms and God in deistic terms. "But you as a priest help me find another way to look at life," said this executive.

When those words were first spoken to me, I had just finished seminary and was searching for my own identity in this new vocation. The resources I had to work with, on his challenge and mine, were the Biblical tradition, a few pastoral skills, and a consciousness of God. The point is that I did have another way of looking at life to offer, and it was the firm foundation for identity.

Our identity lies ultimately in our calling to be sacramental people. One of the great themes in the Biblical tradition is that God is in the world creating, sustaining, and redeeming the possibilities for life against the threats of chaos and personal despair. We are called to be sensitive to those possibilities and to help one another actualize them, to come to peace with the life process and see God in it. We become sacramental people, outward and visible signs of Christ's incarnation and involvement with us and of the power of his resurrection and his reign as Lord of life. Using our consciousness of God and an evolving understanding of the life process, we are called to help people discern God's active presence in their lives, creating the possibilities for living more wholly. Using the talents or skills we are given and enjoy, we are called to help others overcome the obstacles in their own lives and develop the skills to actualize their possibilities. How much our institutions teach us to be engineers and executives; how little they teach us to live. Thus we exist to celebrate God's power among his people. And, of course, through all this process we discover life for ourselves. For our ministry is not a role but a lifestyle characterized by how open we are to God and how free we are to respond to life. As a result we are the church in the world, and this world

includes both where we work and our parish, wherever the faith
is still in the process of creation. Albert Mollegen, in my ordination sermon, said with his usual wisdom that we are called to be
midwives of the Spirit.

The second question, about the impact of the job on our
experience of God, recognizes that we are an experiential people;
what we experience is what we believe. One of the great gifts of
my job is that I continue to encounter creation and the life process
in an ever-renewing way. I cannot describe or explain the
experience but I can point to it through another's words: "Viewed
from the distance of the moon, the astonishing thing about the
earth, catching the breath, is that it is alive . . . Aloft, floating
free beneath the moist, gleaming membrane of bright blue sky . . .
the only exuberant thing in this part of the cosmos."[4] Creation: its
ambiguity as life-giving and as threat, as pregnant with meaning
and devoid of meaning, but never to be taken for granted. That
searching is our life style. It follows that, as a problem-solving
people responding to new opportunities to live, we are in the
process of becoming. Instead of seeing man and woman in
Promethean terms, I see us as a people being drawn ideologically
toward Teilhard de Chardin's Omega Point or whatever form the
Day of Yahweh takes. I can sense it because I am participating in
it. I can sense through my work the evolution of man's awareness
and community. And this evolution or eschatological event is
happening also on a day to day basis as people discover and fulfill
their own personhood.

As for the third question, on the options for ministry, they are
as multitudinous as the life situations and the people with whom
God brings us into contact. If Christ calls us, and the Church
blesses and commissions us, it is the people who give us our
ministry.

At work we are missionaries witnessing to the immanence of
God. As missionaries we also correct the stereotypes of faith,
church, and ministry through our presence and dialogue. We can
provide counselling services, expanding the awareness and skills
of people in areas of life cycle development and personal relationships. With our sensitivity and skills in community building, we
can help task-oriented groups deal with group process and develop
supportive relationships. We can develop small groups among

Christians that nurture secular holiness; i.e., personal religious life, supportive relationships, and ways of ministry on the job. We also have the power to be heard in decisions affecting our people, not because we are ministers but because we participate in the decision-making process.

In the parish, we can bring supportive relationships to our brothers and sisters. One of the working concepts in my job is the buddy system for life support. Not being directly involved in the politics of the parish, we can also be non-threatening support systems to our rector and he to us. This is one of the great joys in my own parish, and, given the loneliness of clergy, a gift not to be underestimated in its mutual value. The rector is the principal shepherd in his mission field, the parish, and I am shepherd in mine. He keeps me effective in mine, and I help him in his.

It seems to me that the worker minister has three broad job possibilities: 1) as a full-spectrum pastor in charge of a small church, 2) as a generalist assistant to the rector helping carry the full range of responsibilities, or 3) as a specialist for a subculture such as the young or aged or as an educator or counsellor. The skills required are equally diverse. He can bring a sacramental awareness that encourages people to live in the world more confident in the presence and activity of God. He can bring to the community's life organizational development skills and an understanding of the political process. He can help deal with working people's questions and all the questions of the power game. He can help people see their jobs as places to help others who have to deal with such struggles.

Let me close by saying that I have learned an awe and respect for creation, the possibilities of life, and the gifts we have to realize these possibilities. The ambiguity of creation has been resolved by the living Lord present in this ministry in a way that gives courage to live and act in the face of the mystery. We share confidence and sensitivity with others in ways that make life possible for them. We thus celebrate the presence of God's power. Our spirits reach out in prayerful love to encounter him. His presence grows within us. We are in union with him. He dwells in us and we in him.

11.
A WORTHWHILE MINISTRY IN ITSELF

Neilson Rudd

Father Rudd is a geologist primarily concerned with underground gas storage reservoirs who lives in southern Illinois and is in charge of the Episcopal churches in McLeansboro and Centralia.

Some months ago I was collecting core samples at an oil drilling operation when one of the workers mentioned with some amusement that there was an Episcopal priest in McLeansboro, Illinois, who had the same name as I. He wanted to know if we were related. It happens that we are very closely related, for I am he. Chronologically, my first profession is geology. I am a consultant primarily concerned with oil and gas producing reservoirs and underground storage facilities. But I am also vicar of St. James, McLeansboro, and priest-in-charge of St. John's, Centralia, two small congregations in southern Illinois in the Episcopal Diocese of Springfield.

How did I come to this dual function? First of all, I am not sure it is in fact a *dual* function, in the sense that my two professions are separate. To the contrary, they have merged to a large degree. I have found that I cannot divorce my priestly role from my secular activities. People with whom I come in contact in the business and scientific world frequently call upon me for pastoral and spiritual advice. Our common secular interests seem to break down a barrier to communication. And certainly my knowledge and experience as a scientist and businessman contributes to my priesthood, as in fact it contributed to my entering Holy Orders.

I was baptized in the Episcopal Church and attended several churches with some regularity during my childhood, but otherwise managed to avoid any religious training or commitment until my early twenties. As I began to perceive more of the order and beauty of the universe through my scientific studies, I found it necessary to accept the notion not only of a Creator, but of a Creator who cared. From this toehold of faith, one necessarily has to contend with all of the other questions which logically follow. So rather against my natural inclination, I became increasingly interested in theology. Exactly how and when I made the transition from intellectual inquiry to Christian faith is unclear. It was something more than a decade in the doing and was certainly influenced by a number of individuals, particularly my wife.

During this period of intellectual and spiritual wandering, we were also wandering geographically from our origins in upstate New York through several military stations, to graduate school in Minnesota, to a research position in Washington, D.C., and ultimately to the oil fields of southern Illinois. Primarily as a result of my wife's more active churchmanship, we had contacts with the Episcopal Church during most of this period, and a few years after settling here I found I could say the Creed without crossing my fingers and prepared for confirmation. Over the next few years I became increasingly active both in our local congregation and at the diocesan level.

Since the Diocese of Springfield includes many missions and just over a dozen economically stable parishes, the diocesan mission budget can never provide enough mission clergy. There are hundreds of members of the church who suffer de facto excommunication because they live too far from existing stations. There are many small mission congregations which have grown stagnant for lack of spiritual and pastoral leadership. There are congregations that have lived so long on the verge of financial disaster that they have come to see their whole reason for being as survival rather than the extension of Christ's ministry. Yet all of these, with a minimum of inspiration and leadership, have the potential for becoming important and effective centers for the church's work in southern Illinois.

On several occasions I had considered the possibility of a priestly vocation but had put it off as being inappropriate for one who still wrestled with God too frequently, and as impractical for one whose children were approaching college age and who had other business and personal responsibilities. As I became more convinced that I was called to the priesthood, another problem arose. If I were to follow the normal course of seminary training, my business contacts would be severed, probably irrevocably, and I would become dependent upon the ministry for my income. That would not contribute to solving the problems of the small missions for which I had developed a special concern. Happily, at about this time our diocese decided to consider the possibility of locally trained deacons and priests. In my case this simply meant that the readings in theology, history, and scripture, which had continued since my renewed interest in the church, took on a more formal and diversified nature under the direction of several priests.

Local training, primarily by home study, is not an ideal situation, particularly in a diocese which is of mixed emotions about the desirability of such a course of action and has no well-defined curriculum or standards of proficiency. I am very much aware of gaps in my knowledge and proficiency, although these gaps narrow as I gain experience and continue my studies. But on the other hand, the smaller missions are not particularly demanding in many areas of the ministry. My knowledge of church music is poor, yet in a small congregation the few good singers contribute more scattered through the pews than concentrated in choir stalls and, when the organ has chronic emphysema, the musical abilities of both organist and priest matter very little. The same is true of liturgics. The Sunday Eucharist, infrequent Evening Prayer services, and the occasional Pastoral Offices in a small church are not very demanding and, on those few occasions when something special comes up, advice is readily available from other clergy in the area.

If there are deficiencies in what I can bring to small congregations, there are perhaps also some compensating strengths. I know, understand, and like small towns and their people. Unlike many young mission priests, I do not see serving these small congregations as a necessary "internship" through which I must pass in my professional career as a priest. To me it is a satisfying and worthwhile ministry in itself. I don't want to run a mini-cathedral but rather to help people to know, worship, and express Christ in their lives in whatever context is appropriate. With twenty years of business experience behind me, I have some expertise in working with people and in administration. I prefer dealing with people as individuals rather than as groups.

I can preach an adequate Sunday sermon, but I suspect I do much better at our coffee hours, parish suppers, discussion groups, and in the living rooms and kitchens of my parishioners. The same is true of church school. While we do have a church school program, I am sure that at least as much gets done in frequent, less formal contacts. In short, I rejoice in a luxury which is not possible for many priests, the opportunity to adopt each of my parishioners as family in practice as well as in name.

What does this do to the congregation? It relieves a great deal of stress and releases a lot of creativity and love. Perhaps one really has to live in a small mission as an involved layman fully to understand their position. Small mission congregations are highly committed people; were they not, their churches would not survive. They are dedicated to the church. They are faithful in worship and support, often sacrificially so. But for all their commitment, support, and sacrifice, their existence is precarious. It takes all of their ability just to maintain a status quo, to pay what they can of a priest's stipend, and to carry the minimum overhead of maintaining a church building. There is but very little leadership, time, or money left over for the real work of the church, the extension of our Lord's ministry. Further, mission priests come and go, each contributing from his strengths and abilities, but with little continuity. And there are frequent and sometimes long intervals when the congregation must do without clerical leadership, relying upon occasional supply priests. This is not a growth situation. The congregation cannot undertake a forward-looking program, knowing that with the least shift of the wind, with the resignation of a priest or the loss of one or two substantial pledges, the program must be cancelled and possibly the mission closed. Certainly it would take a remarkably committed person to join a congregation whose future was so uncertain.

Since my ordination, I have served four congregations, one continuously, two for periods of a few months, and one for eight months at this writing. These four congregations represent virtually the full spectrum in size for our diocese. Each has responded differently to my period of service, but thanks be to God, I think none has suffered and some have grown in service to our Lord.

St. James, McLeansboro, was at the point of being closed when I was assigned there shortly after my ordination to the diaconate. Only two or three faithful but elderly souls attended services early on Sunday mornings, an hour made necessary by the fact that St. James was served by a priest from a town some thirty miles distant. For the same reason, the priest could spend little time in the community. Many residents of McLeansboro thought that the church was closed. With my assignment to St. James, we were able to change our hours of service to a more convenient time, making it possible for Episcopalians from the surrounding area (up to thirty-five miles away) to attend regularly. One young couple who had been interested in the Episcopal Church elsewhere returned to McLeansboro and were soon confirmed. Another young family who had been attending services in another community due to the limited program at St. James, decided to return. This injection of youth into the congregation encouraged the older members, and growth has been continuous ever since. We are still a small mission, less than forty souls, but we are ministering outward in the community and in the diocese rather than being ministered to.

In my other mission assignments, I have been in positions normally staffed by full-time, stipendiary priests, twice on an interim basis, and now on a semi-permanent basis in another. To these congregations I think I have represented hope, continuity, and a breathing spell. Hope, in the sense that my appointment shows that the diocese is responsive to their needs; continuity, in the sense that I try not simply to "supply" but to assume a role of pastoral coordination if not leadership; a breathing spell, in the sense that for a time their financial burdens are lifted so that they can figuratively and literally put their houses in order, paying off indebtedness and undertaking needed repairs and improvements. For a brief period, at least, they can catch up and go ahead, rather than always running to keep up. In no case has a congregation taken advantage of my non-stipendiary ministry to reduce its giving in its mission budget. On the contrary, they have increased their giving, sometimes very substantially, and have contributed more to the diocese and other works of the church.

The increased commitment of dollars has in all cases been matched by an increased commitment of time on the part of the congregation. Among other things, they are aware of the limitations on my time; that I cannot be janitor, coffee hour host, and church school teacher, as well as priest and pastor. I suppose there is also something in my example, for they know my ministry to them is in addition to my full-time secular occupation. Beyond holding regular services and calling on the sick and needy, anything that the congregation wants to happen will take place only when they make it happen. And they do. Aside from the spiritual life of the church, I do not lead or direct; I facilitate and encourage. Within broad limits, the program which the congregation develops is one which expresses their ministry in Christ in the context of their location, their facilities, and their abilities, rather than in accord with some externally imposed model.

And, of course, if I am able to give anything to the congregation which I serve, they have given me infinitely more. They have been patient with my inexperience, responsive to my needs, enthusiastic and cooperative when things are going well, and open and candid when there are problems. Serving Christ through them and with them is a joy beyond description. To be part of a family in Christ which is emerging from the threat of economic and pastoral crises, from the cramped position of being thrust into a mold which doesn't fit, and which is finding that, under God and with the gifts of the Holy Spirit, it is an asset to Christ's church rather than a liability, is an exciting experience.

Where do I go from here? I don't really know. Gradually I am disentangling myself from some of my secular commitments to be able to devote more time to mission congregations, but I do not foresee giving up the non-stipendiary character of my ministry. Presumably some of these mission congregations which mean so much to me will eventually need a priest with more pastoral skills and more time than I can provide. But I am sure that in my lifetime, we will not be without these struggling missions which need just a little gentle cultivation to blossom forth.

12.
THE MINISTRY OF INSURANCE AND SKIING

Edward Hook

*Edward Hook is an adopted Coloradan who combines
being a life insurance agent with being in charge of St.
John's Episcopal Church, Breckenridge. He resides in
Colorado Springs.*

At the age of twenty-five I got out of the U.S. Army and entered
the life insurance business as an agent. For two years I remained
in this position, liking it. But I found I was searching for a still
deeper meaning in life. Through the Episcopal Church, I met other
seekers and knowers, and the end result was that I went through
the Virginia Seminary. The experience was excellent, and the
process of learning or developing theological professional care is
a privilege that I wish all could share.

Upon graduation in the spring of 1963, I became assistant at
All Saints Church, Worcester, Massachusetts, later becoming
rector, and subsequently resigning that position in February of
1971 to re-enter the business world as a worker priest. There are
many reasons for my resignation as a full-time clergyman. Suffice
it to say that all I had learned in seminary and at All Saints Church
had prepared me to carry ministry into the marketplace.

My family and I moved to Colorado Springs, where I re-entered
the life insurance business with New England Mutual Life. Being
a skiing family, we also spent weekends in Breckenridge, Colorado,
and I became "continuous floating priest" at the little Episcopal
church in Breckenridge.

It was natural for me to return to the insurance business, having
been in it prior to entering seminary. It is a person-oriented
business, helping people plan and solve financial problems in
areas of premature death, retirement, health, taxation, and saving
money. Anyone who has done any counselling knows that
problems are magnified if financial considerations are added to or

are a part of marriage, job, or other problems. I feel that financial counselling and planning and insuring for the future is ministry, theologically sound, and relationship-oriented. Let me expand a bit on this concept.

The insurance man is in a unique position in that his services are completely free to prospective clients. Only when a product is bought does the salesman earn a commission. In the selling process, many things come to light as one gathers information, verbally and nonverbally, about the prospective client and his family in order to make recommendations about present and future planning. The relationships within the family and financial obligations now and in the future are all integral parts of the planning process.

Basically, in terms of insurance and personal relationships, one of two things happens to a person: he or she either dies too soon, or he or she lives too long. In both instances there can be financial and psychological problems. The job of the insurance man is to help people face the issues realistically and to make plans accordingly. In the case of premature death, life insurance can enable the survivors to make unhurried and reasoned decisions about the future, without being a burden to family or friends.

In terms of retirement, permanent life insurance helps provide the funds, along with Social Security, pension plans, etc., so that the retirement can be fruitful and enjoyable. We all know of persons who did not put enough money aside, and when retirement came they did not have the funds necessary to live in the way that they wished to.

Two other areas are involved. One is "the living death," where a person is temporarily or permanently disabled, thereby losing his or her power to earn needed income. The other area is sickness and accidents. The cost of being sick or injured constantly rises and can spell financial disaster. In either area, thoughtful and realistic financial planning can help take care of the problem, so that the person or his family are not forced into extreme debt.

I spend some time on this subject because I am convinced that it has very real and strong theological matter in it. We are all given life and, in faith, life abundantly. However, living with a firm Christian belief does not mean that there will never be any problems, tragedies, or hard times, along with the joys of life.

Planning realistically for the future — for death, for unforeseen occurrences, illnesses and tragedies, for future income — are all a person's obligation in living responsibly in God's world. We are given a responsibility for what has been given to us, and we are to use our brains in making the large and small everyday decisions which affect our lives and those of others. This is truly Christian stewardship.

My seminary training and my work as a full-time parish priest have been helpful to me in working again in the business world. In fact, they are the foundation of my work now. They put life in perspective, help me see persons as individuals, each worthy in his own right. Being outside full-time institutional church work helps me relate to others without being labelled as the professional whose "job" it is to care. It also helps me understand the hurts and the problems of the people in the marketplace. The average person does not wish to do evil to others, does not want to make decisions which adversely affect others, yet situations arise where the dilemma is very real and the choice hard. To be in the market-place is an asset in counselling and empathizing within this area. People really do minister to others without having an official title put to it. People do develop the capacity to care, and the institutional church is part of the process that enables this action. In turn, the teachings of the church are carried by people into the world, sometimes very quietly, and life is enhanced.

One of the basic reasons for the existence of the church is to prepare persons to live in the world realistically, and to be ministers of the Word to others in the everyday matters of life. If I could name one area where I feel the church has often failed, it is here. The church has not let people go out from its institutional life to become ministers in the world, but rather has worked to keep them dependent, fostering a separate community. The concept of the worker priest is a bridge and a correcting move.

I do not believe that there is an adequate understanding of the worker priest by the church. I see this ministry not as a forsaking of God or religion but rather as an expansion and opportunity to serve in a new way, at least in our day and age. The tie to the institutional church is there, but one is given the opportunity of living out what he has learned and preached.

My work at St. John's Church has been basically to celebrate the Eucharist on Sunday mornings, to counsel and visit, to take care of the needs of the parishioners and help in the community, and to point the people towards themselves in the community of others. St. John's is a very tiny mission in the mountains, at the base of a ski area, so it has a very transient congregation. The people are community-oriented, and visitors from many other places are generous in their support of the St. John's Help Fund, an instrument to help any who are in need. The church has no organizations, no official budget or income, no endowment — just a group of dedicated persons seeing that the job gets done and ministry is carried forth. Perhaps getting organized in the traditional sense would spoil the beauty and ease of St. John's.

Two brief stories will help reflect the worker priest relationship. Soon after coming to Colorado and re-entering the insurance business both in Colorado Springs and Breckenridge and taking services at St. John's, I received a call concerning baptism. I met with the couple and kiddingly said that a requirement for baptism was to look into insurance matters! As it turned out, the father needed financial counselling and has been a client of mine for over three years in many areas of insurance. And the baby was baptized. A good working relationship was established.

Then, on Christmas Eve a year ago, my wife and I decided that there were many people in Breckenridge who were away from close friends and family at that time, and we decided to have a party after the 8:00 p.m. Christmas Eve service. An announcement was made, and about seventy-five persons showed up at our home. An enjoyable time was had by all, and everyone felt at home, not as strangers.

Such things are not the end-all or be-all of ministry, but to my mind the worker priest situation offers an element of freedom to be and to do: to exercise one's ministry in official ministration through a parish, and also to carry ministry and theological convictions into the marketplace.

13.
DOCTOR AND DEACON

Edward A. Downs, M.D.

Ed Downs is an internist in Lubbock, Texas, and a deacon on the staff of St. Christopher's Episcopal Church. He is also an accomplished musician and organist.

In 1969, at the age of forty-one, I first became aware that in the Episcopal Church it is possible to be a self-supporting clergyman and have a ministry that combines a secular occupation with ecclesiastical functions. It is surprising to me that this was so late in coming to my attention, because I had first given serious thought to studying for ordination while in my late teens. At that time, however, a strong interest in natural science and especially in human biology led me to the choice of a medical career.

After four years of college, four of medical school, four of hospital training, and two years of military service, I entered the private practice of internal medicine and diagnosis, in which I am still engaged, devoting to it an average of sixty-five hours per week. This includes hospital rounds, office practice, clinics, meetings, medical study, unpaid teaching at a medical school, consultations, house calls, and emergency room duty.

There is one key person who is predominantly responsible and instrumental for my having been ordained. He is the Rev. Kenneth R. Clark, Jr., rector of St. Christopher's Church in Lubbock, Texas. He dedicated many hours to my training, education, and development for ministry, requested the necessary permission from our bishop, and worked with extraordinary devotion towards my ordination. He continues to guide my growth in the ministry. Other clergy in the diocese also helped me to prepare for the same General Ordination Examination required of seminarians prior to being received into the clergy. Thus local pastors were my entire theological faculty.

As rector of the parish to which I am assigned as a nonstipendiary curate, Father Clark assigns my liturgical responsibilities and works closely with me on the planning and execution of my several other parish activities, including layreader's training programs, inquirer's classes, and Bible study groups. As a deacon, I take the reserved sacrament to homes and hospitals for the communion of the sick and disabled. Plans are in progress for my ordination to the priesthood within a few months.

In my medical practice, I am aware of an increasing involvement in Christian ministry. This becomes evident in questions and problems presented to me by patients, nurses, and co-workers in the paramedical field. As the knowledge of my special interests and ordination spreads, I receive comments, inquiries, and expressions of interest that invite statements of witness and commitment on my part, as well as opportunities to give information on the content of our faith. Seeing me on pastoral calls in a clerical collar elicits rather dramatic responses from those who otherwise have known me only as a physician. The Episcopal "presence" in this highly fundamentalist area in which we live is in itself a matter of interest and perhaps challenge to many people I encounter.

There are many profound implications for any Christian person who must frequently confront death and dying, questions of abortion, prolongation of life in the terminally ill, transplantation counselling, and such problems of medical ethics. I learn from patients and families, crisis situations, and discussion groups, at the same time that I try to convey the comfort, guidance, and hope that the Gospel provides. I have also had the rare experience of conducting a funeral service for a long-time patient who made this request of me in the final days of a prolonged battle with cancer.

There is an interesting relationship between my secular work and my church functions. Many of the people in my parish have been under my medical care and thus know me in two roles. It is therefore impossible for me to have two "selves" that remain separate and distinct from each other, and a real attempt at integration becomes necessary. I must be ready to discuss medical subjects at church functions and theological matters in my medical office if the situation and need require me to. In a recent office counselling session with an unwed mother-to-be, I was asked, "What do you think of this as a priest?" and such occurrences bring it home to me that I do not "wear two hats." Instead, I have a single ministry in response to a call from God, who has led me into multiple channels of expressing his will for my life. Indeed, these channels include not only the ordained ministry and the medical profession but also being a husband, parent, son, citizen, and friend. I try to keep from feeling torn apart by the variable, often intense, demands that my life makes upon me, hoping with God's help to mature and progress creatively. I believe that God, through his grace, has granted me some successes as well as an increased ability to deal with my failures.

In a subtle and somewhat distinctive way, I believe that my presence in our parish life, as a tentmaker, has something to say to the congregation about the ministry of the laity. The man in the pew realizes that I am fully ordained and yet also closer to being a layman like himself than is the case of the full-time clergyman. Economically, socially, and psychologically, I have the same stresses in the world that he has. I am a living example of the fact that laity and priesthood are "combinable" in the same person — that the priesthood of all believers is not necessarily a mere abstract idea. This does not prevent the congregation from recognizing my specialized liturgical and sacramental functions, rejoicing in them with me and sharing the benefits of such abilities as my theological training has developed in me. I like to point out that a layman does not cease to be a layman when he is ordained deacon, and he remains both layman and deacon when ordained priest, each order of the ministry having special functions and duties within the whole body of the church. In this setting, I do not hesitate to attend laymen's conferences and functions as well as those designated for clergy.

My relationships with other clergy in the diocese have been cordial and accepting. It is still either too soon or too difficult for me to know what their true inner feelings may be towards my ministry and ordination, in part because I am the first locally-trained tentmaker in the diocese, and they have had nothing on which to base impressions in the past. My own reaction towards other ordained persons is one of brotherly comradeship and sharing.

Finally, I believe there will be a growth of the self-supporting ministry, in terms of numbers, usefulness, and effect on the total life of the church. I speak favorably and encouragingly about it whenever I can. I welcome the opportunity it has given to me and cherish the enrichment of life it offers.

14.
AN INDUSTRIAL MINISTRY

Father John Aschenbrenner, S.D.S.

Salvatorian Father John Aschenbrenner is a quality inspector on the Briggs and Stratton line in Milwaukee, Wisconsin, and assists in St. Anne's Roman Catholic Church.

As I was walking away from the assembly line after making my line check, a worker drove his forklift near me and stopped. He leaned back against the lift and asked, "John, do you know where I can get a better job?" I asked him what he meant. He said, "I hate this job. Sometimes I feel like if I have to drive this thing one more day, I'm going to ram it into the wall. And if I get married and have a kid, then I'm stuck here the rest of my life."

Most of the time my work is routine, like the work so many other people do in the factory, but occasionally I find myself confronted with questions like the preceding one. It is during these times that I am most aware of my ministry as one of accompaniment in a factory setting. Before I explain what I mean, I would like to give my background and why I decided to work in industry.

I received a degree in mechanical engineering from Marquette University in June, 1959. My engineering education included visits to and summer work in several Milwaukee industries. After graduation I began work at Sperry Utah Engineering Laboratories in Salt Lake City; however, after a few months I informed my supervisor that I was leaving work to prepare for the priesthood.

I entered the Society of the Divine Savior (Salvatorians) and was ordained a priest in Washington, D.C., in 1967. Soon after, I received a Master's degree in Religious Education. In 1969 I left for the missions in Tanzania, East Africa. There I did parish work and directed seminarians in the Diocese of Nachingwea. However, after two years in Africa, I felt the missions were not my place and decided I would return to the States to stay at the end of my three-year contract.

I spent many hours of my last year in Africa thinking about and planning for the future. I am uncertain when I became interested in a ministry in industry. I knew that a couple of Salvatorian priests were industrial chaplains in England, where 150 other priests and ministers were involved in industry as chaplains. Since I felt ineffective when ministering in ecclesiastical settings and since liberation movements were signs of the times, I thought it was time to liberate myself from traditional ministries. A ministry in industry, as I was beginning to understand it, was a very attractive alternative, although I was not sure what form it should take. I thought possibly I could be a chaplain with an office in a factory, where I would counsel workers with social and/or religious difficulties. It was clear to me that my ministry should not involve me in conflicts between labor and management (both labor and management have sophisticated machinery for that), nor should it involve me in making converts. Another possibility would be for me to get a factory job and simply work along with the other workers. I concluded that whatever form this ministry would take, it would enable me to do something I felt was very important, i.e., to be self-supporting rather than being dependent on others.

When I returned from Africa, I spent about a year in a parish. During that time I went to Detroit for an interview with Ford Motor Company. The interview seemed to be a failure. I had prepared to present my ideas simply and clearly. Yet my ambivalence was apparent. I wanted to work in industry, but as priest, and yet I was unable to speak with complete conviction about wanting a chaplaincy because somehow I felt a chaplain could easily become removed from the reality industrial workers live with, and so from the workers themselves. Nor could I talk with much conviction about working at a regular job, because I could not see clearly how a priest could do this and still be fulfilling his call to minister. The director of hourly personnel told me in so many words that Ford was not interested in establishing a chaplaincy, because it would mean staffing it with ministers of all denominations. However, if I was interested in a job on the line, he was sure I could get that. I went home confused and angry and depressed. Yet the interview was worthwhile. It helped me clarify for myself what shape of ministry I was going to pursue. I contacted the director of placement at Marquette University. After several visits with him and his resource people, I decided to set aside the idea of a chaplaincy and look for a factory job. My hope was then to find a job that would give me the opportunity to relate to fellow workers and at the same time to do some pastoral work informally. Mr. Panlener at Marquette put me in touch with the Briggs and Stratton Corporation, a large manufacturer of small motors in Milwaukee. In a brief interview with the vice president in charge of engineering, my idea of a priest working in industry was understood and accepted. After checking my references, the company hired me. I began work in July, 1973.

My job is simple. Sometimes I inspect the assembly of motors and at other times the production of parts to see that they meet specifications. Workers do a lot of talking before, during, and after work, on breaks, and at lunch. Our conversations are usually about jobs, cars, sex, politics, etc., but some concern religion and other matters of personal importance. I have had opportunities for counselling on an informal basis and for the administration of the sacraments.

The wage I receive is not only adequate for my own support but also enables me to contribute to the support of my community. I am also able to do the parish work I had hoped to. I celebrate masses and visit homes in St. Anne's parish in Milwaukee without depending on the people for financial support.

How do I see the work I do as ministry? I learned that the core of the Catholic faith is that God is "kindly disposed" to all persons, as Jesus showed by his life, death, and resurrection, and that we are affected by this kindly disposition. As Jesus showed the kindly disposition of God to persons of his time, so we Christians are to show it to persons in our time. I think that this can and should be done *in both secular and ecclesiastical institutions*, because I believe that the spirit of God moves not only in the church and its sacramental realities, but also in the world and its natural concerns, drawing the whole of humanity anywhere and everywhere into friendship.

In the work that I do and the relationships that I have with other workers, I have many opportunities to give and receive kindly disposition and friendship. Any Christian leadership I exercise among them depends on how well I work with them, how much of a human being I am among them, and how well I live my belief in Jesus and his teachings among them, many of whom have different beliefs and values than mine. However, more important, I have come to appreciate the fact that my work is not really so much a matter of leading and following as it is one *of accompanying.* I try not to tell other workers what to do and not to do, what is good or what is not. I simply exchange greetings, help a fellow worker move a load of parts, share food and drink, talk and laughter, as well as do my job. All these personal exchanges make work more than just work. Therefore it should be apparent that work that is more than just work means ministry to me. This ministry is one of accompanying others, being with them, in whatever they are experiencing at work. I found Pope John so appealing because I saw him ministering from Rome by accompanying us through life.

This ministry is entirely worthwhile to me. I can share in people's lives both in the church and in industry. Both places of ministry offer me the variety and novelty of experiences so helpful for my own spiritual renewal and for keeping my feet on the ground. Still, I need support in this ministry. I would encourage anyone interested in it, provided he has some liking for industrial work and the people who do it. I welcome associations with ministers of other denominations. Ministers from different backgrounds could bring to bear a fuller articulation of the meaning of Christian life and work. I would also welcome the understanding, acceptance, and promotion of the worker ministry and its value both for the church and for society by both church and industrial leaders.

15.
PRIEST-BAKER IN LONDON

David M. Wilson

*David Wilson is a baker in Camberwell, a section of
London in the Diocese of Southwark, and an area supervisor of worker priests for the diocese.*

When the Bishop of Southwark, the Rt. Rev. Mervyn Stockwood,
announced a plan to train priests by the then-unheard-of method
of night school, a door to the ministry was opened in England.
Not only was this an opportunity to recruit fresh, hitherto
untapped manpower, nor simply a new method of training, but
also a new, but really a very old, form of ministry.

There was in England at that time a small group of priests who
had chosen to leave the parochial ministry for full-time secular
work, spurred on by the experience of the priest worker movement on the continent, which the bishop was not only aware of
but had seriously been promoting as an idea in this country for
many years. The response to the bishop's appeal passed all
expectations. The Southwark Ordination Course was formed
and began work in September, 1960.

Then a lay reader in a parish in the heart of Brixton, I joined
the course in September, 1961, and after many struggles and a
great deal of hard work, passed and was ordained deacon in the
diocesan cathedral in 1964. I had passed nine examinations since
leaving full-time education at the age of thirteen, a considerable
achievement. I also spent fifteen weekends a year and my entire
holidays for three years in residence in the courses. During this
period I had not lost a day's work (the baking trade is a six-day
week), and on the Monday after ordination I was back in the
bakehouse, not knowing what lay ahead or even what sort of
animal I was meant to be within the Church of England. I felt
even more odd subsequently because of considerable local publicity
about my dual career.

Two points became very clear at the outset. One was the awareness of seeing God outside the church building and in every situation, highlighted by the need to be completely honest and trustworthy. Second was the sudden realization that people began to see me as a spokesman for the church, or Christianity. Whereas as a layman my ministry was limited, now as a priest I found myself exposed to all the questions, not only of help, love, and care, but of morals, money, and prayer.

Being a priest in secular work means exposure to the pressures on a practicing Christian, close to situations where sharp practices are taken for granted, and conformity to low standards of morals and ethics are not only accepted but expected. The parish priest may well call from his pulpit for the need to live the Christian life at work, but he is seldom faced with such things as being offered stolen goods, cheating the management of time, "perks" which are really straightforward thefts, or the chance to "fiddle" the tax inspector by huge expense accounts. It is in this field that the priest worker finds his greatest challenge and the least amount of support or even intelligent discussion within the church.

Because of these pressures, plus the effort of sixty hours a week in the bakehouse with all that is entailed in the management of a small family business, I have always limited the amount of time I am prepared to give to the parish. As a deacon I had to be licensed in one parish, and for the first two years gave it my full support, but carefully limiting my time. It is so easy to be caught up in the machinery of meetings and other activities while the family, recreation, and reading gradually slip away.

In my third year I was pushed into taking over a daughter church in difficult circumstances, and I found the regular opportunity to celebrate and function as a priest to a small group very beneficial to my own soul but totally inadequate for the needs of the people and the community they lived in. Time restricted the work to maintaining the worship in the parish and essential visiting of the sick. Because the group was weak to begin with, we made no real impression on the community and no growth in the Christian church.

In 1968, after various consultations, a Chapter of Priest Workers was set up in the diocese to offer support to the growing number of men in this field. This was again an innovation within the

Church of England, and the men elected me as their first dean. This job gave me the right to attend the Bishop's Deans meeting, to represent the men to the bishop directly, and to offer support to any priest worker in difficulty. Without exception, every case I dealt with in four years concerned the relationship between the priest worker and the incumbent to whom he was licensed. I gave up the daughter church and received a license from the bishop to preach anywhere in the diocese. I held four meetings a year for the priest workers, as well as visiting them and getting to know their secular work and their parish setups. I also initiated a study by King's College, London, into the theological working of the chapter in particular and the priest worker movement in general. The paper that was then written is just beginning to see daylight.

At work I have to make decisions quickly which affect my staffing, production, work relationships, and my profitability. I am trained to think and act while taking into account the effects of my actions. When I come up against the parish structure, I find indecision, lack of purpose in dealing with such straightforward matters as drains, guttering, painting, etc. In a meeting of clergy to deal with current matters of theology, there is a sense of not knowing what the church is about.

The parish priest sees the priest worker as a threat to his position, simply because he has a foot in two camps and can speak the language of both sides. As the church is forced to move more and more into a position where clergy and laity are seen to be a team, with the same objectives but different functions, so it will become easier for various experiments in ministry to take place. It is to be hoped that this will happen naturally.

In sum, the last fifteen years have seen such a radical alteration in the whole structure of ministry (and in many senses the debate is only just starting) that there needs to be time for the study of the theological side of the issues as well as for reflection. As it is, the pace of life today and the speed with which one event (the rise in the price of world oil) can have shattering effects upon every nation, is taking the church along with it. It may well be that having among the clergymen in trade, industry, and professional life will save the church from being totally submerged and give it a voice to speak to the world which could not be obtained in any other way.

MINI-HISTORIES

16.
MORE THAN A POLICY

Father John Blossom, C.L.U.

The Rev. John D. Blossom is a general agent for Provident Life & Accident, a pension consultant, and in charge of St. Stephen's Episcopal Church in Peoria, Illinois. The following article is adapted from the August, 1970, Review *of the Provident Life & Accident Insurance Company.*

A self-supporting priest who is a pension consultant is how the Rev. John D. Blossom, Jr., C.L.U., describes himself. John is in charge of St. Stephen's mission parish in the inner city of Peoria, Illinois, and is a principal of Small, Parker, Ackerman, Blossom, Inc., general agents for Provident Life & Accident Insurance Company, specializing in retirement programs.

"I am an Episcopal priest because I feel that is what God wants of me, and I sell retirement programs because I enjoy it and it allows me to live the way I choose. I don't receive a salary as a priest."

John says he sees no conflict between being a priest and being a successful pension consultant. "My sales outlook," he stated, "helps me to be a more effective communicator. Pension work helps people over sixty-five to live with dignity. I consider retirement plan sales and consulting an important form of ministry."

A member of the Million Dollar Roundtable since 1971, John anticipates no trouble in maintaining his membership while functioning as a priest. "A small parish like mine (which has about sixty people) doesn't require a full-time conventional priest."

In addition to working on the design of new and revised retirement programs and performing service work for the firm's more than 150 corporate clients, John has a full schedule as a priest. His week begins Sunday at his parish church, where he conducts the service and usually gives the sermon. Weekday evenings may include counselling a couple prior to marriage, meeting with an adult study group, or participating in a community activity. The normal business day often includes church-related calls and meetings and hospital visits with friends or parish members.

"My wife, Susan, and our two children, Jay and Amy, are very understanding. Because my hectic schedule prevents our being together as much as we would like, we try to emphasize the quality of our family activities." Among the activities they enjoy are sailing; unless a wedding or a crisis intervenes, they can be found on a nearby lake Saturday or Sunday afternoons during the summer. John has been active for years in his community and in the industry and doesn't believe that his newly acquired priesthood conflicts with these activities. "I feel very strongly about this 'whole man' concept, and my activities with the Human Relations Commission and other organizations within my community and in the industry contribute to my being a 'whole man.' These activities are part of my ministry."

John emphasizes one point firmly. "We really shouldn't try to separate our religious lives from the way we live from day to day. The way we operate as business and professional men says more about our religious commitments than what we do — or don't do — Sunday morning."

17.
GOD AND HOWARD JOHNSON'S

David Hogarth

Episcopal Deacon David Hogarth combines being chaplain at the Suffolk County Jail in Boston with being personnel coordinator at the national Howard Johnson's headquarters. This interview is adapted from the December, 1974, Brown Alumni Monthly. *(Since then Hogarth has been appointed Coordinator of Cooperative Education at Wentworth College of Technology in Boston.)*

David Hogarth, Brown 1960, walks at a crisp pace, hopping down from curbs and skipping up again on the other side of the street. On the subway, he leaps up to offer his seat to a woman carrying a load of packages, saying, "I still believe a man should be a man, even though I know it's illegal nowadays." David Hogarth is, among other things, the chaplain for the non-Roman Catholics at the Suffolk County Jail in Boston, and he never stops running.

Although his jail ministry is his primary job, David Hogarth is one of the "tentmaker clergy" who make their living by working outside of the church. He is the personnel coordinator at Howard Johnson's national personnel office in Wollaston, Massachusetts, where he does "people work" — that is, anything which "assists the employees profiting the bottom line" in areas such as job descriptions, compensation plans, and employee relations.

Working under the "Orange Roof" is actually an extension of his ministry, David feels, because it allows him to reach many more people than he could through the church. "Twenty-four thousand employees in forty-two states are our babies," he says. "People ask me why I don't go into the ministry full time — but this is *all* I'm doing. It's a unique ministry with a small 'm'."

Besides God and Howard Johnson's, David Hogarth is big on several other causes. He is active in fund raising for the Boston

Ballet, the Massachusetts Bay United Fund, and above all, Brown University.

Originally a pre-med student at Brown who later majored in French, David decided to become a minister because of his experiences at the Episcopal Church on campus. When he walked into St. Stephen's, Providence, for the first time, he says, "The sanctuary was blue with incense. It was a spiritual orgasm for me." In 1968 he began working at the Suffolk County Jail. "A large part of my ministry is actually to the guards," he says. "Everyone thinks I am a chaplain to the prisoners, but the staff is also part of my concern."

David is critical of the criminal justice system in this country because so many people are denied their Constitutional right to a speedy trial. "Our society has forgotten about justice for those behind bars," he says. He is also outspoken about job discrimination practiced against exoffenders and has started a parolee employment program as an outgrowth of his work with the Personnel Managers Club of the Boston Chamber of Commerce.

18.
ENGINEER-PRIEST

John F. Hird

John Hird is senior staff engineer for Western Electric Company, East Baltimore, and rector of Trinity Episcopal Church, Howard County, Maryland. This interview was done by Newburn Jones in The Washington Post.

"The world is filled with men and women who are required to expend their efforts on work which is meaningless, soul-destroying, degrading or harmful to their physical beings," says the Rev. John Francis Hird.

Father Hird, a "worker priest" who lives in Linthicum Heights, is rector of Trinity Episcopal Church in Howard County and senior staff engineer for Western Electric Company.

"As an engineer-priest, I spend a large portion of my time in scientific-engineering-management pursuits in industry, consulting in the field of quality control which deals with worker efficiency," says Father Hird.

"As quality control technology advances and I search for new knowledge, I find myself scouting the frontiers associated with the very qualities of work itself and their theological implications," he says.

Father Hird, a University of Rhode Island and Maryland Diocesan School of Theology graduate, says he became interested in the quality of work and subsequently religion when he was working on a banana plantation in Latin America.

"We were in the business of loading bananas, and I was trying to find a more efficient way of doing it," he recalls. "In my observations, I found that there was a very close correlation between work efficiency and attitudes of workers. My work with the banana industry also brought an awareness that I was being given the ability to see something that was in existence, and that I was given the means to be the first man to describe this to people in a way they could understand," says the minister.

During his twenty years at the huge Western Electric plant in East Baltimore, Father Hird has come up with some innovative thoughts about man and his work, and he has had an opportunity to travel to Japan and Western Europe, as well as throughout the United States, to explain them.

"We put people in factories and try to get maximum efficiency from them, not concerning ourselves with people as human beings but as machines, and this is where we make our mistake," he says. "When we begin to see the people who run these machines day in and day out as individuals with inner feelings, we begin to increase their awareness of themselves and of others. The worker develops a sense of worth," says Father Hird. "He is happier, and everyone around him is happier because everyone feels his own worth."

"Man has certain needs and aspirations," he adds. These needs and aspirations can be separated into three life-systems. Father

Hird calls the first system the Intellectual-Spiritual (IS) system. This system involves the human activities associated with developing complete openness among individuals, permitting uninhibited creative adaptability in order to give human life meaning.

The second system, the Sociological-Political (or SP) system works towards developing an effective social interaction which provides a perfected governing relationship among all men for the common good. Finally, the Economic-Technical (or ET) system "allows man to develop his capability for utilizing his physical universe so that all men live becomingly and without waste."

These three systems must balance each other out, says Father Hird, but he adds, "Our industrialized society has made the ET system the control system for measuring human progress, drawing on the energy of the other two systems only when it appears that we can gain some short-term advantage by doing so."

Father Hird contends that this imbalance has led to many changes in modern man's patterns of social behavior, particularly those involving his attitudes towards work and younger workers.

"We have spent billions of dollars to improve the quality of our public education, and as a result the outlook of the average younger worker is quite different than it was in the past," says Father Hird. "He aspires to different things than his parents and grandparents. His hopes, dreams, and expectations are much higher, and because of this he is less willing to accept things as they are. He wants some life out of his work," he adds.

The fifty-one-year-old priest was born in Boston, and he and his wife Virginia were married in 1945. They have three children: ages twenty-eight, twenty-two and seventeen. They will soon be moving into the Trinity Church rectory at 7474 Washington Boulevard.

An officer in both the U.S. Navy and the Merchant Marine during World War II, Father Hird spends his time in more direct religious pursuits when he is not lecturing or working on a new scientific publication. He insists that his dual roles as an engineer and priest are inseparable.

"The real beginning of my conscious awareness of the reality of God came to me through my work as an engineer," he says. "I feel that I was given a special perception to share the vision of the

Creator with other people. We are all members of the Body of Christ, and the rest of the world is calling for us to bring his life to them."

19.
A SHOCK TROOPER ON THE FRONT LINE

William Cary

> *Bill Cary is an Episcopal priest and in public information*
> *with the Georgia-Pacific Paper Company, and priest*
> *associate at St. James's Church, Lincoln City, Oregon,*
> *and St. Barnabas, Portland. This profile is adapted from*
> *an article by Rachel Sullivan in* The Downtowner,
> *Portland, Oregon.*

Bill Cary has two full-time jobs. He is not moonlighting — both employers know about the other job. His combination of jobs is unusual: he is a minister in the Episcopal Church as well as being assistant director of public information with Georgia-Pacific.

"This is often called a tentmaking ministry," said Cary. "It's a comparatively new thing for the Episcopal Church, but it goes back to the original Apostles. Many of them were tentmakers or fishermen at the same time they were preachers."

Cary made the decision to become a minister after a long career as business editor of the *Oregon Journal.* His training for the ministry was not the usual seminary experience; he attended night and weekend school for five years.

Cary's current full-time job in public information doesn't mean that Cary is a Christian after hours. "It's not as if I'm a weekend minister who puts his collar on during the weekend," said Cary. "I am not a Christian reservist — I'm more like a shock trooper out on the front line."

"Everyone who knows me is aware I am a minister," said Cary. "Sometimes that means people have to get to know me before they can treat me like another person. At first there is this hesitancy to be around me. The feeling is, 'Gee, I can't cuss in front of him.' "

"The feeling is too bad," commented Cary. "Hopefully, when they discover I am person enough, they won't be afraid of me."

Cary makes no conscious effort to let people know he is a regular guy. "The only thing I can do is just be me," he said. "I have my own foibles. I cuss when I close the door on my finger. I know I shouldn't, but I do. When people find out I am not a Puritan, they can come to me, knowing I am not going to damn them to hell."

As Cary's co-workers have come to accept him, some have come to him for counselling. "I have become the chaplain of the sixth floor," said Cary. "I am kind of an outpost to the church. Many of the people who come to me would never go to church — not because they would be afraid to; it's just they would never think of it."

Cary acts as a listening post, but he also makes no bones about having his own message. "Punch a preacher and you'll get a sermon," he jokes. But Cary has an interesting commentary on how Christianity fits into the 1970's.

"A lot of people rejected Christianity when they were young and never think to look at it again. Maybe they had a bad Sunday School teacher, or they got turned off by being sent to Sunday School when their parents stayed home. For one reason or another, they've turned their backs on Christianity.

"But we all need to feel not alone, and people end up looking for religion elsewhere, in Hare Krishna maybe, or a meditative religion. They look for something exotic. Their feelings about Christianity are that they have been there already, and the grass looks greener on the other side of the fence.

"My contention is that they haven't really given Christianity a chance. Christianity is not the pedantic thing it's sometimes made out to be; there's no religion more mystical and Eastern than Christianity. Where did Christianity start, after all?

"And, of course, one of the first precepts in Christianity is 'love your neighbor as yourself.' Sure it's hard to love your neighbor when it means the wino who hits you up for a quarter. But a one-to-one concern for other people is what makes a human world out of an uncaring one where we lose sight of people.

"Hopefully, people who are looking for answers to basic questions will think about Christianity. Even if they had bad vibes
when they were young, maybe they'll take another look."

20.
JUST LIKE THE LAYMEN'S TIME-BIND

Richard Thew

*Dick Thew is vicar of St. Thomas's Episcopal Church,
Canyon City, Oregon, and vice principal at a local high
school.*

The following is my non-stipendiary story. The idea of many
members of the Episcopal Church is to hire someone — the
clergy — to do their Christianity for them. My idea was to put
the clergyman into the same kind of time-bind that the typical
layman has to deal with. This would make the clergyman more
aware of the problems of the laity and force tha laity to do their
own Christianity.

I was educated to be a teacher in secondary schools. I taught
for two years and then I chose to go to seminary. I attended the
Episcopal Theological School in Cambridge, Massachusetts, and
was ordained following graduation. My assignment in the Diocese
of Eastern Oregon was to be vicar of St. Thomas, Canyon City,
a small rural mission. The congregation had always needed help
to pay for its clergy. The first year I was in Grant County I was
supported by the minimum salary minus whatever I could earn at
part-time work. I worked as a service station attendant, heating-
oil truck driver, and as a substitute teacher. The second year I
became a teacher, counsellor, and vice principal at a small local
high school. I have been earning my living at this job for five years.

I worked hard to help the people of Grant County understand
this new ministry. They could no longer expect the vicar to make

weekly visits or schedules at any time of the day. They had to learn to do some of these tasks by themselves. It was a slow process, but we slowly worked closer to our goals. After five years, the work of the church is mainly carried out by the laity. I function as a priest sacramentally, and as an enabler and resource person. Counselling has been shared by myself and other resource people in the community. The diocese has provided backup resources in the form of people and material to provide training to our congregation.

Much of the calling on the sick, the needy, and families of members is done by laypeople. The buildings are supervised and cared for by the laity. We have two buildings: the church and the parish hall. There is an active day care center operating in the parish hall. It takes a lot of work on the upkeep of the building, not to mention the volunteers, teachers, and others who put in their time. Planning and organizing social events and study groups have been handled by the laity. Small groups of all kinds have flourished, died, and been replaced by others. Many activities have taken on an ecumenical framework to make the most of the resources of the churches in the community. Layreaders have been very active. This latter participation also promotes the idea that laity can and should take a regular part in the worship of the church.

Of course, all has not been roses. More than once we have planned a dinner or some other function only to arrive and find that nobody had taken charge and set up whatever was needed. It has been a successful ministry, however, because of the dedication and cooperation of the members of St. Thomas's family. They have grown in their knowledge and understanding of the Lord and the life he wants them to lead.

21.
RETIREMENT?

Ellis Clifton

Ellis Clifton, Sr., is a retired armed forces officer serving as non-stipendiary assistant at Trinity Episcopal Church, Detroit.

Before my retirement in 1970, after twenty years of service with the U.S. Marine Corps, my job assignment was in the field of public relations. As a counsellor to the families of servicemen, I dealt with cases which involved problems of pay allotments required to give service families support when a Marine leaves a base for overseas duty. My job was to see that the families were left with everything they needed, such as housing, medical care, commissary, and a church home. My office kept in close touch with the base chaplain because there was also a need for his services.

I then worked in the Army Tank Automotive Command, from which I retired a second time in 1972, to begin working full time at Trinity Church, Detroit. My job assignment at ATAC was in the cataloguing division, where all automotive equipment, including blueprints and data that were used to assemble a vehicle, was researched for a technical manual to be used by troops in the field. There were visits to be made to automotive companies to get data for this manual, because they were contractors for the vehicles. This job required public relations experience and automotive training. I was given an extensive six weeks course in public relations in Washington, D.C.

While working in the 1960's, I had been taking classes at the school of theology of the Diocese of Michigan. I was graduated from the school, and in December, 1968, was ordained a perpetual deacon at Trinity Church, Detroit. My presenter was the late Father Schuyler Clapp, Sr.

Until my retirement from the Army Tank Automotive Command, I worked part-time assisting at Trinity. My job assignment was to assist in the conduct of worship, make parish calls and hospital visits, and be involved in all the church programs. Upon my retirement from the Army, I was enabled to increase my work assignment at Trinity under the Rev. Schuyler Clapp, Jr., assisting in establishing a number of programs: a youth program, PAL program, Operation Friendship for the mentally retarded, and others. Later, Father Clapp left Trinity for another responsibility, and I was in charge for one year. During that time I baptized twenty-two persons and presented thirteen for confirmation. All of these people were drawn to Trinity by my program of neighborhood visiting. The other programs of the church have continued to grow in terms of participants and community involvement. My counselling experience and public relations training (both gained while working in secular work) have greatly assisted me and strengthened my ministry. For the past two years, the Rev. Frederick B. Jansen[5] has been in charge of the parish. He has started summer programs for the youth in the community, and my responsibility this past summer was to organize and coordinate the educational experience for the fifty children involved in this program. I have enjoyed working with Father Jansen very much, because he permits me to exercise my ministry fully and assigns me to tasks that are challenging and require growth. These are pastoral calls and counselling which involve my weekdays. I administer the business affairs of the church and attend many meetings in my district and in the diocese. My work assignment also involves relating Trinity Church to its community.

22.
PRIEST/COLONEL IN THE LINE

William Komstedt

The Rev. William A. Komstedt, Jr., is a regular Air Force colonel and assistant at St. Christopher's parish in Midwest City, Oklahoma. This mini-history came from the pen of Mrs. Eleanor Hamilton of the Episcopal Diocese of West Virginia.

Jobwise, Bill Komstedt is the only priest in the United States Air Force who is not a chaplain but a regular Air Force colonel currently assigned as a deputy chief of staff/operations for Headquarters Southern Communications Area. His organization is responsible for providing communications-electronics services at Air Force facilities throughout the southern half of the United States.

Churchwise, Bill is an Episcopal priest of the Diocese of West Virginia, having come into the diocese in 1972. The Bishop of Oklahoma has assigned Bill to assist at St. Christopher's parish in Midwest City, which serves the military community around Tinker Air Force Base and Oklahoma City Air Force Station. In addition, he helps the Diocese of Oklahoma provide a ministry at St. Francis Mission, located in a poor inner city neighborhood near the state capitol.

How did Bill get into this work? During off hours while serving as a career officer in the Pentagon, he helped Episcopal chaplains at the Veterans Hospital in Washington as a layreader. There he found he had reached the limits of lay ministry. In dealing with patients, he became acutely aware of the need for sacramental authority to celebrate the Eucharist, to administer the sacrament of Unction and to pronounce Absolution. These motivations became, finally, a clear call to Holy Orders. It was through the help of the Rt. Rev. Wilburn C. Campbell, Bishop of West Virginia, that Bill had his opportunity to study and finally achieve his goal as a priest.

Bill sees his role as a non-stipendiary priest primarily as augmenting the installation chaplain's program, to provide a sacramental ministry to Anglicans where it is not otherwise possible, and to provide an Episcopal witness. The role of "tentmaker" or worker priest in the Armed Forces is new. At this point he says he "wouldn't swap places with any chaplain or civilian clergyman in existence."

"There is a special rapport which exists between me and our military families because of the mutual missions we share both for the Air Force and the church," Bill declares.

23.
MEMBER OF THE NON-STIPENDIARY CORPS

Elwood Cridlin

M. Elwood Cridlin is a semi-retired labor relations consultant and a roving non-stipendiary for the Episcopal Diocese of West Virginia out of Huntington. Again we are indebted to Mrs. Eleanor Hamilton for the case history.

Prior to retirement as a railroad labor relations executive in 1971, Elwood Cridlin was engaged in all types of railroad collective bargaining, adjudication, mediation, etc. Upon retirement he devoted much of his time to two Episcopal congregations in which he was most interested: one a large city parish, the other a small diocesan mission. It was suggested that he study for Holy Orders, and in due time he was ordained deacon and priest. Being in a retired status, he has greater freedom to act or fill in than if he were still in regular employment. This status has been enjoyable. Elwood says that his ordained status has in no way adversely affected his secular status. He now does some labor relations work for a single small client. He believes his secular work and experience have been of particular value to him in functioning as a priest.

He feels that the situation in West Virginia is special in nature, and that "a well-trained non-stipendiary corps can be of genuine value in maintaining and expanding the Blessed Gospel here." Such a corps, he continues, "cannot be expected and should not be expected to take the place of the carefully and well-trained priests from our seminaries. There should be no competition between the two types. Each should see its place and do its best to fulfill its obligations. I am honored to be part of the non-stipendiary corps as of this time."

24.
THE MARKETPLACE AND THE VINEYARD

Dr. Rex J. Hartley

*Dr. Hartley is a West Virginia podiatrist and a priest
assistant at Trinity Episcopal Church, Morgantown. His
experience is again related by Mrs. Eleanor Hamilton.*

Dr. Hartley has been a doctor of podiatry for twenty-five years
and was ordained to the priesthood over a year ago. Both his jobs,
he says, were motivated by experiences during his early years. As
a child, he was plagued by a foot problem which was treated
successfully by a podiatrist. As a youth, he had the good fortune
to come under the guidance of a fine Christian church school
teacher and he decided he wanted to "know the Lord as she knew
him." Although Rex felt that the Lord called him to Holy Orders,
such aspirations, he says, were pushed aside by three years service
in the United States Navy during World War II.

After the war he became a doctor, "but really floundered with
God," being in and out of five or six different churches searching
for redirection in his spiritual life. "The answer," he says, "came
in the Episcopal Church, where ultimately the Lord again spoke
to me and rekindled the fire of my youth." He enrolled in the
West Virginia School of Religion, and while this school was
designed primarily for the training of laity, some of its graduates
have continued onto the priesthood, as Rex did.

The most frustrating part of being a non-stipendiary priest,
Rex says, is allocating the time he would prefer to use for his
priestly functions. He serves on the staff of Trinity Church in
Morgantown and assists the rector in many ways: celebrating
Mass, teaching, making hospital calls, student (Morgantown is
the home of West Virginia University) and other counselling, and
being a supply clergyman in his convocation.

"I find that my ordained state has a profound impact on many
of my patients," Dr. Hartley says, "and I am becoming increasingly

more involved with their spiritual ills as well as their physical problems." He notes some reactions. "One patient informed me that she thought it absolutely wrong for a priest to forgive sins. Another, noting the ashes on my forehead, was shocked to learn that we Anglicans received the imposition of ashes just as do Roman Catholics. Because of the unusual opportunities to be a witness to the Lord in my office, being a priest has made me a better doctor, and being a doctor has made me a better priest."

Rex complains that his secular job does get in the way of his ministry and he must constantly discipline himself to keep his priorities in order between the marketplace and the vineyard. "I am self-employed; I am non-stipendiary. I do have a wife and children to care for, so if I am to work at all in the vineyard, then I must be productive in the secular world. Holy Scripture is quite unclear how St. Paul managed his tentmaking business and his missionary journeys at the same time, but I do take heart in the fact that the Lord uses all things for good, even a non-stipendiary priest."

EPILOGUE

James L. Lowery, Jr.

Ministry studies is a fairly new interdisciplinary area of investigation. One might think of it as a tasty stew composed of one part sociology of occupations, one part psychology of careers, one part management and administration studies, and one part ecclesiology and missiology. Be that as it may, it is my home field and, I believe, one which can offer some helpful insights and guidelines after one has read through the introduction and the case histories in this book.

TERMINOLOGY

Various terms have been used to describe the style we call "tentmaking": worker priest, bi-vocational person, self-supporting minister, non-stipendiary clergyman, minister-worker. No single sobriquet has gained universal primacy. This book has put the term "tentmaker" in first place because of its fairly recognizable Biblical origin. Paul the Apostle earned his way around the Mediterranean world on his missionary journeys by making tents in the marketplace (as with Aquilla and Priscilla in Acts 18). He did what we would call *church ministry on top of a secular financial base*. Hence a tentmaker clergyman is defined as an active, ordained clergyperson in good standing who combines a church position or assignment with earning a major part of his/her compensation from sources outside the church.

SPREAD, TYPES AND PROFILES

In a series of studies growing out of the National Council of

Churches Clergy Support Study of 1974, Robert L. Bonn[6] and others ascertained that twenty-two percent of the clergy in nineteen selected mainline denominations fall into the tentmaker category as we have defined it. Bonn distinguishes two groups of tentmakers: the *part-timer* (thirteen percent) who is in a secular job twenty to forty hours of the week; and the *moonlighter* (the other nine percent) who is in secularly-remunerated work one to twenty hours a week. His point is that the motive for the secular work of the part-timer is financial support for the church ministry, while the motive for the moonlighter is additional challenge (and ministry, we add) on top of the church position. He sees the profile of the moonlighter as more similar to the full-time professional pastor, while the part-timer often labors under the handicaps of an inferior educational background (compared to the moonlighter), less opportunity for continuing education, and being located in a sparsely populated area at a distance from resources.

Jud, Mills, and Burch, in their significant study *Ex-Pastors,*[7] looked at over 400 United Church of Christ pastors who had left full-time pastorates for other positions. Most of these positions seem church-connected, in that they are either non-parish church-work or, if they are secular jobs, those holding them are also free to accept church responsibilities. It was noted that these individuals are relatively better educated, better paid, and more aggressive and self-initiating persons than their counterparts in the full-time pastorate.

A look at deployment figures in the last few years in the Episcopal Church (EC), the United Presbyterian Church in the United States of America (UP) and the Presbyterian Church in the United States (PCUS)[8] adds further illumination. There has been a decline in communicant members in all three denominations. The median size of congregations in 1972-73 was below the level to provide for full-time professional pastors (EC 175 communicants, UP 178, PCUS 126). The largest number of vacancies by far were in congregations below 200 communicants. Personal research in the Episcopal Church, plus helpful reports from the denomination's Clergy Deployment Office, tell us of continuing vacancies in almost five percent of the denomination's congregations at the same time that there is a clergy surplus for full-time pastors in the Episcopal Church. These vacancies, in other words, are in places so small and weak that the compensation would not even allow a full-time pastor to starve!

Our conclusions from these sets of data are threefold. First, mainline denominations simply could not operate in many jurisdictions without the constant support of and use of tent-making clergy. Second, there is a great variety of types of tent-makers. And third, there are tentmakers who excel in skills, education, and ability. Tentmaking not only need not be, but in most cases is not, a second class ministry. It involves, where rightly done, very skilled practitioners.

A way to classify tentmaker clergy is by educational background. Some of them, as noted in the case histories, have come into their present style of ministry via the residentiary graduate seminary route which has been common in the last 150 years. But another group has stayed in secular positions while being prepared via judicatory[9] programs, never leaving their secular jobs, and being ordained in place, so to speak. Holmes's estimate in the introduction to this book is that this group constitutes about one-third of Episcopal candidates for the ministry. In the Roman Catholic Permanent Deacon Programs, this latter group constitutes almost 100 percent of the candidates. The issue here seems to be whether or not the preparation shall be deemed first class, and at least the equal of a seminary education. A look at the Washington-Richmond program, for example, in the Roman Catholic Church, will show that equality in education can be achieved.

Another way to type tentmaker clergy is by the method of their recruitment. Some have recruited themselves; we suspect it to be the largest group. Others have been recruited by the clergy and hierarchy. And a final, very significant group, especially large and noticeable in the Episcopal Diocese of Alaska, are those recruited and elected from the congregation by the local congregation whom they will serve.

One thing worth noting about mature and locally based candidates for the tentmaking ministry is that their selection is more easily and surely done. The persons are established in the community. Their capabilities and characters are known. And they are proven in community involvement. An interesting statistic in the Episcopal Diocese of California (San Francisco Bay area) is that twenty percent of the old-style clergy have marriages which are breaking down. But none of those of tentmaking clergy are. We are dealing with mature persons who have proved their capability in leadership, judgment, stability, and communications skills. Many of them bring management and administrative experience which makes them strong in areas where many seminary-trained pastors are weak. One of the readers of the first draft of this book, Dr. Carl Dudley of the McCormick Theological Seminary in Chicago, notes that Robert Bonn (in the studies mentioned above) declares that tentmakers with management and business backgrounds are more willing to become rectors and senior pastors in charge of parishes than are tentmakers with counselling skills and background as chief strengths. Dudley sees the case histories in this book as corroborating Bonn's analysis. He further notes how the majority of the tentmakers belong to the executive and professional class in outlook and training. He sees this as a significant shift from the unsuccessful attempt in France in the 1940's and 1950's to recruit persons of worker background to be worker priests. He concludes that the experience of the case histories herein tends to show that the ordained ministry is in part a profession requiring a certain level of ability and approach to service. Indeed, in this context we must mention the Anglican Diocese of Hong Kong, a pioneer in having a whole judicatory run largely through the use of the tentmaking ministry, where the policy is to recruit tentmakers from the professions. The diocese seeks out such persons as teachers, sanitary engineers, lawyers, etc., because they are already tuned in to one-to-one service relationships, skilled in communicating knowledge to people, and have the kind of control over their schedules so that they can more easily juggle ecclesiastical and secular responsibilities.

On the other hand, one experienced source in England feels that secular employment in the crafts or at the working-man level leaves more psychic energy for the ecclesiastical function. Perhaps our baker-priest case history fits in here. Also there comes to mind a statement by an acquaintance, "I can tie flies because I'm good at it. This gives me the financial opportunity to do the ministry I am called to." There is something to be said for this view.

THREE CRITERIA AND A GUIDELINE

What some readers will be searching for are guidelines as to what factors make for tentmaking ministries that work. The case histories which go before show that "tentmaking ministries do fly." But what criteria can we draw from them for enabling future new ministries? We believe there are at least three.

The first is the criterion of creativity. That tentmaking ministry will work most creatively which combines the secular and ecclesiastical functions most fittingly into one ministry. David Hogarth's chaplaincy work with prison guards and his personnel work at Howard Johnson's become one ministry when you enter the Red Coach Grill on Clarendon Street in Boston and find that the bartender at that Howard Johnson-owned eatery is a former prison guard disabled on duty who needed a part-time job to supplement his insufficient disability pension. Or lawyer Bob Sharp (not represented in these case histories) combines practicing criminal law in Kansas City and serving a parish in nearby Overland Park. He finds that much of his pastoral counselling is done in his law office, and that his law office is the place to follow up much of his parish work. Two functions, one ministry. Where this can take place we are onto something very, very creative.

Second comes the criterion of liveability.[10] Where the place of residence, place of job, and place of church ministry are widely separated, life is extremely difficult. Such was the case with Harry Woggon in his first of three ventures in tentmaking. Where two of the places are on the same turf, the situation is much better. And where all three are combined in one area or neighborhood, as with the doctoring, deaconing, and residence of Edward Downs in one neighborhood in Lubbock, Texas, the result is excellent.

Third comes the criterion of targetability. Another way to look at the tentmaking ministry is in terms of its focus. If the target of the ministry is a congregation, then the filling of the secular position should be done in a manner to leave opportunity for meeting parish emergencies. The secular job had better be one in which the person has some real control over his hours. If the focus of ministry is a neighborhood or a community, then a different style is needed, such as being both high school guidance director and congregational pastor to enable a community family ministry.

One further guideline should be added. A key to a successful tentmaking ministry may be in beginning where there is already status and acceptance. The tentmaker plays two roles, one ecclesiastical and the other secular. One of them should already be established, a means by which he/she is already recognized as a person of character and authority. Then the other half of the arrangement can be acceptable, strange though it may seem initially to the neighbors, onlookers, and assorted gossips. Hence Gene Patton was established as pastor before he took on work as a librarian. And Fran Schwannecke was known as an honest person who would rent anything under the sun to Saginaw people before she was ordained and began work with senior citizens. Here is a diplomatic strategy for carrying people with you in spirit as you move into a tentmaking style.

ISSUES

The tentmaking ministry raises some prickly issues that must be faced.

The first issue is that of the time-bind. Several of the case histories touch on it. How does one resolve the conflict between the demands of job, family, and church position? Several things must be said. To lead off, tentmaking requires a disciplined and organized — or else a most open and flexible — person to deal with its various demands. The kind of arrangements described above, where the church and secular functions often dovetail, complement, or meld into one, can be set up so that often the tentmaker is gaining time by killing two birds with one stone. Witness the guidance man in a school district who is the parish pastor of the same area and whose family counselling sessions may cover both functions at once. In this way he may accomplish forty hours of secular work and twenty of pastoring in fifty hours, not the sixty hours that would seem to be required. And finally, there must be willing cooperation on the part of the family. Most Roman Catholic permanent diaconate programs wisely do two things. They contract for a commitment of, let us say, fifteen hours of time per week, both during the preparation period of two to five years and also after ordination. Thus by the time of ordination it is known whether or not the candidate and his family can handle the time demands. In addition, the spouse's official consent is necessary before a man can enter the program. Very often the response is, "Why, he's already spending that much time in church! Go right ahead; it's no problem."

The second issue is whether tentmakers are to be considered

first class or second class citizens. Where a more "catholic" view of orders/ordination prevails, the former is the greater possibility. But this is counterbalanced by circles within which first class status as a clergyman is in effect equated with both a graduate residentiary theological education and a full-time church position. An example of the anomalous position in which tentmakers may find themselves is the fact that the Episcopal Diocese of Utah passed a resolution at its 1975 convention classifying "sacramentalist" clergy among the laity for purposes of voting and serving on commissions, while the Episcopal Diocese of Alaska counts them among its clergy order. A practical example of bad treatment is the setting of meetings for clergy at times when secularly employed persons can never attend. Opposing this is a growing practice, in such places as the Episcopal Diocese of California, of scheduling clergy meetings on Saturday, at which time both secularly employed and full-time church servers can be present.

A third issue is that of accountability/responsibility. The tentmaker is not controlled as much by the ecclesiastical institution. He has more outside financial resources. He thus has greater freedom vis-a-vis the local church board and the judicatory superior than a clergyman entirely dependent on the church for his income. This situation requires the board and the executives to persuade the pastor into a voluntary agreement, and given the change in dynamics here, this can be a very threatening thing for them. On the other hand, there is the question of the tentmaker's responsibility and accountability. The tentmaker often comes to his dual vocation by a process of entrepreneurial search, selling, and negotiation. He has a greater freedom. He has a secular excuse to say "No" to church responsibilities. And this can be misused. The question is whether the self-supporting minister will be an undisciplined "free bird" or whether he will be responsible and place himself under a voluntary discipline.

A fourth and final issue is perhaps the most important of all. For it deals with the basic mission of the church. The modern resurrection of the tentmaking ministry has usually been connected with the problem to too many, too small churches on the one hand, and insufficient support for full-time clergy on the other. The issue therefore is whether the Christian Church will see tentmaking as a cheaper way to keep the same old ship afloat, or whether it will see it as a God-given source of renewal and a means to "multiply the ministry of Christ."[11]

Our position on this issue is that the return to this style of ministry represents a creative renewal out of the deepest roots of Christian faith and practice. It offers countless new opportunities to minister to small groups, in special settings, and to meet new needs without tying such mission and ministry to an expensive institutional package of salary, buildings, etc. The watchword to be associated with the tentmaking ministry is "opportunity." May this model and style once again flourish as a valid way to minister in the way of Christ. It works. It overcomes the separation between secular and religious. And it offers a magnificent opportunity.

NOTES

[1] Robert L. Bonn and Sheila M. Kelly, *Clergy Support Study of 1974* (New York, National Council of Churches). Also, Robert L. Bonn, *Analysis of Clergy Support Study* (Richmond, Society for the Advancement of Continuing Education in Ministry, 1975).

[2] Roland Allen, *Missionary Methods: St. Paul's or Ours* (Grand Rapids, Eerdmans, 1962).

[3] Conrad Bonifazi, "Biblical Roots of an Ecologic Conscience," in Michael Hamilton, ed., *This Little Planet* (New York, Charles Scribner's Sons, 1971), p. 205.

[4] Lewis Thomas, *The Lives of a Cell* (New York, The Viking Press, 1949).

[5] Both Father Clapp, Jr., and Father Jansen have served Trinity as seminary-trained non-stipendiaries, earning their living as professors at Wayne State University.

[6] Robert L. Bonn and Sheila M. Kelly, "Secular Employment of Protestant Parish Clergy," paper delivered at Fall, 1974, meeting of the Society for the Scientific Study of Religion-Religious Research Association, in Washington, D. C. Also Robert L. Bonn and Ruth Doyle, "Secularly Employed Clergymen: A Study in Occupational Role Recomposition," in *Journal for the Scientific Study of Religion,* September, 1974.

[7] Gerald Jud, Edgar Mills, and Genevieve Burch, *Ex-Pastors* (Philadelphia and Boston, Pilgrim Press, 1970).

[8] a. Distribution and Deployment of Clergy in the Episcopal Church 1968-72; Clergy Deployment Office, Episcopal Church, 1973.
   b. Personnel Study, Donald K. Campbell, Division of Professional Development, General Executive Board, PCUS, 1974.
   c. Report to the 1974 General Assembly; Personnel Services, the Vocation Agency (UPCUSA).

[9] Diocese, district, conference, synod, etc.

[10] As defined by Dr. H. Boone Porter of Roanridge Institute outside Kansas City.

[11] This term again comes from the pen of the Rev. Dr. H. Boone Porter in a statement entitled "Multiplying the Ministry of Christ," which was issued by a group of 150 Episcopal clergy and laity meeting in the basement of St. George's Church, Kansas City, Missouri, over Memorial Day, 1969, and disseminated throughout the denomination as a means of changing the canon law of that communion with respect to unpaid ordained ministries.